ROBBER TO REPENTANT

The Life and Sayings of Abba Moses the Strong

Introduction, commentary, and translation by
FR. JAMES NESSIM

Robber to Repentant: The Life & Sayings of Abba Moses the Strong

Copyright © 2023 by Fr. James Nessim

All rights reserved.

Designed & Published by:
St. Mary & St. Moses Abbey Press
101 S Vista Dr, Sandia, TX 78383
stmabbeypress.com

10 9 8 7 6 5 4 3

Contents

Abbreviations	v
Foreword	vii
Preface	viii
A Note On The Texts	xi
1 Introduction	1
2 The Times of Abba Moses	12
3 Who Was Abba Moses?	26
4 Spiritual Struggle In the Wilderness	35
5 The Life of Abba Moses	61
6 The Sayings of Abba Moses	84
7 The Seven Instructions	114
8 Hymns	117
Doxology 1	117
Doxology 2	119
Psali Adam	121
Psali Watos	123
Antiphonary	130
Melody	137
Another Melody	142
Salutations	146
Bibliography	149

ABBREVIATIONS

ABC	Wortley, John. *The anonymous sayings of the desert fathers: A select edition and complete English translation.* New York: Cambridge University Press, 2013.
Abbé Isaïe	Regnault, Lucien. *Abbé Isaïe. Recueil ascétique: Introduction et traduction française par les moines des Solesmes.* Bégrolles: Abbaye de Bellefontaine, 1970.
BSAC	Bulletin de la Société d'Archéologie Copte
Budge	Budge, E.A. Wallis. *The Paradise of the Fathers V. II Containing the Counsels of the Holy Men and Questions & Answers of the Ascetic Brethren Generally known as the Sayings of the Fathers of Egypt.* London: Chatto & Windus, 1907.
Bustān	Bishop Epiphanius. *Bustān ar-Ruhbān.* Cairo: St Macarius Monastery, 2014.
CE	Coptic Encyclopedia

Conferences	C.S. Gibson (trans). *Nicene and Post-Nicene Fathers, Second Series*, Vol. 11. Edited by Philip Schaff and Henry Wace. Buffalo, NY: Christian Literature Publishing Co., 1894.
GCAL	Graf, Georg. *Geschichte der christlichen arabischen Literatur*. 5 vols. (Studi e Testi 118, 133, 146, 147, 172). Città del Vaticano: Biblioteca Apostolica Vaticana, 1944-1953.
Give me a Word	Wortley, John. *Give me a Word: The Alphabetical Sayings of the Desert Fathers*. New York: SVS Press, 2014.
More Anons	Wortley, John. *More Sayings of the Desert Fathers: An English Translation and Notes*. UK: Cambridge University Press, 2019.
PG	Patrologia Greaca
PO	Patrologia Orientalis
Vita di Mosè l'Etiope	Pirone, Bartholomew (ed., and trans.). "Vita di Mosè l'Etiope." *Studia Orientalia Christiana Collectanea* 24 (Cairo–Jerusalem 1991): 7–115.
Lausiac History	Clarke, William Kemp Lowther. *The Lausiac History*. London, 1918.

FOREWORD

St. Moses the Strong has, for hundreds of years, etched out a place of historical honor within Coptic Orthodox Christianity, because of the strength of his heart forged by His love of God. Although he was killed by the sword, his life persists and his legacy pervades to this day, with a multitude of places of worship and Coptic gatherings bearing his holy name, aside from his mention at the altar and in our hymns and songs.

The St. Mary & St. Moses Abbey Press, named after the holy mother of God, and the beloved St. Moses the Strong, is privileged to publish a work of this scholarly caliber from the author of this book, providing us, for the first time, an English translation of the Arabic biography of this saint's life.

This is a book that will allow us all to gain insight into the strength of heart of St. Moses, learning about his life not only out of intrigue and amusement, but to serve as an example and inspiration for us to embrace an intimate spiritual life with God, no matter where we are in our spiritual walk today.

May the intercession of St. Mary and prayers of St. Moses the Strong be with us, to deliver us from all spiritual warfare and lead us throughout the way to salvation.

God bless you,
Metropolitan Youssef
Coptic Orthodox Diocese of the Southern U.S.A.

PREFACE

I am delighted to present in this modest book the life and sayings of a remarkable saint whose biography alone inspired my own Christian journey. Listening to the stories, miracles, and the intimate connection my friends shared with Abba Moses encouraged me to examine for myself why this saint was so important and a patron to many.

My investigations first began in September of 2022 whereby I was asked to share a word on the life of Abba Moses with the youth of my local parish. I must admit, the title of this book was also inspired by the youth who organized the topic! Several youth members shared their most beloved stories from his biography. Seemingly, two themes formed the crux of their love for him: struggle and forgiveness. They saw Abba Moses's struggle against his passion as their own and his ability to avoid the judgment of another as a means to his experience of divine forgiveness. One youth parishioner said, "I feel a little closer to forgiveness every time I read or listen to his biography." It occurred to me that the biography of Abba Moses moved many to pursue greater depths in their repentance and challenge their current spiritual condition.

One book led me to another, and I finally stumbled across the 14th-century Arabic version of Abba Moses's biography. I found this version to be a unique representation of how Coptic monastic communities during the late medieval period envisaged the character of Abba Moses and preserved his memory. It became very evident that this biography, at least for the monks, was more than just another saint story. Centuries after Palladius and Sozomen, the biography became adapted as a pedagogical anchor by which monks could remain confident in the work of Christ and the movement of the Spirit in overcoming their passions. I attempt to highlight some of these methods in the coming chapters. Nevertheless, there is much to be learned from his biography, and this book by no means claims to have accomplished all that, not even by any stretch of the imagination. I offer to the reader the surface and flesh of a fruit, leaving the reader to discover the seed; to take it, and plant it in good soil.

I ask the reader not to feel intimidated or drawn away by the footnotes, referencing, and all that would seem "scholarly." Academia is not my intention. But for the sake of crediting those who have labored before me, as well as to benefit those who wish to read more, or even to motivate the multi-linguists who prefer original sources, it is thus necessary to acknowledge the appropriate notables.

I owe my gratitude to the community at St Mary and St Moses Abbey Press who were supportive throughout the entire publishing process. The transformation from document to book is not a simple conversion, but requires much training, intricacy, and patience. Their commitment is nothing more than a labor of their love for Christ and His Church.

A NOTE ON THE TEXTS

The *Sīra*[1] (biography) presented here appears in a 14th-century Arabic manuscript held in the Coptic Museum in Cairo. It was published in Italian by the scholar Bartholomew Pirone in 1991 who brought together several Arabic manuscripts containing *Sīrat al-Qiddīs Mūsa al-Aswad* (The Life of St. Moses the Black), ordering them into three families (or groups) of Arabic manuscripts.[2]

He gave the first group the identification *Codex C–P*. The primary text of this family is kept in the Coptic Museum and is catalogued as 'History 469.' The *life* spans ff. 362r–368v. It was copied in approximately the middle of the month of *Barmūda* in the year 1079 AM (end of April, AD 1363), or, according to another date in Coptic, from the year 1076 AM (AD 1360).[3] This manuscript is known as *MS C*. It is one of the most important sources for the biography in the Copto-Arabic tradition because of its dating and content.[4] The second manuscript of this family is housed in the *Bibliothèque Nationale de France* and is catalogued as Arabe 154.

---

[1] The 14th century text translated here will be henceforth referred to as *Sīra*.

[2] *Vita di Mosè l'Etiope*, 7–115.

[3] Georg Graf, *Catalogue de manuscrits arabes chrétiens conservés au Caire* (Biblioteca Apostolica Vaticana, Città del Vaticano, 1934), 266. Cf. Marcus Simaika Pasha, *Catalogue of the Coptic and Arabic Manuscripts in the Coptic Museum, the Patriarchate, the Principal Churches of Cairo and Alexandria and the Monasteries of Egypt*, vol. 1, (Cairo, 1939), 50.

[4] Bishop Makarios, *al-Qawī al-Qidīs al-Anbā Mūsa al-Aswad* (Cario, 2006), 6.

The foliation is ff. 79r–93r. Yūsif ibn Mīkhā'īl is the recorded copyist who completed his labor on the 10 *Ṭūba* 1320 AM (AD 1604).[5] This manuscript is known as *MS P*.

The second group of manuscripts are classified as *Codex B–M*. The primary text of this family is an 18th century manuscript preserved as "Hagiography 620" in the *Bibliothèque Orientale Université Saint-Joseph* (Beirut). The biography spans ff. 70r–75v.[6] This has been given the identification *MS B*. The other manuscript is at the Franciscan Centre of Christian Oriental Studies of Muski (Cairo) and given the catalogue number 28. The life ranges ff. 111v–114v and dates to 1 June 1746.[7] It is given the identification *MS M*.

The last is an undated (possibly 18th or 19th century) manuscript kept in the Library of the University of Göttingen under MS Arab 114. The life spans ff. 216r–227v.[8] Pirone has classified this as *MS G*.

---

[5] Gérard Troupeau, *Catalogue des manuscrits arabes; première partie: manuscrits chrétiens, tome I* (Parigi, 1972), 128; *GCAL* I, 532.

[6] Louis Cheikho, "Catalogue raisonné des manuscrits de la Bibliothèque orientale. V. Patristique, conciles, écrivains ecclésiastiques anciens, hagiologie," *Mélanges de l'Université Saint-Joseph*, tome 11 (1926): 276.

[7] William F. Macomber, *Catalogue of Christian Arabic Manuscripts of the Franciscan Centre of Christian Oriental Studies* (Cairo, 1984), 7.

[8] Hrsg. von Wilhelm Meyer. Bd. 3: Universitätsbibliothek. Nachlässe von Gelehrten, Orientalische Handschriften. Handschriften im Besitz von Instituten und Behörden. Register zu Band 1 - 3. Berlin: Bath, 1894. (Verzeichniss der Handschriften im preußischen Staate 1, Hannover, 3), 371-372. Gawdat Gabra pointed out that the same version was also found in a manuscript housed in the library of *Dayr al-Suryān* under no. 308, which dates 1314. Cf. Gawdat

I am satisfied with Pirone's edition and so relied on his publication of *Codex C–P* for the biography translated here and have followed the same numbering. There are no English translations of the manuscript on which Pirone based his edition, therefore this translation will be the first and preliminary, ready for improvement. To provide a somewhat rounded construction of Abba Moses, there are references to various texts that reflect several traditions throughout this book.

The biography of Abba Moses is first witnessed in Palladius's *Lausiac History*, Sozomen's *Ecclesiastical History*, and the *Apophthegmata Patrum*. These are indeed the foundational sources to the composition of the later Arabic *Sīra* as well as hymns composed in the late medieval period. Tradition flourished from the 4th century onward within *Wādī an-Naṭrūn* and gradually began reaching surrounding regions in Egypt and abroad.[9]

Another important source is the *Ascetic Discourses* of Abba Isaiah of Scetis, who recorded the advice Abba Moses had instructed the monks.[10] They are translated in this book from Bishop Epiphanius's

---

Gabra, "Dair Anba Musa al-Aswad: das originale Baramus Kloster in Wadi al-Natrun," *BSAC* 36 (1997) 72–73.

[9] Tatjana Starodubcev adequately covers the various traditions: "St. Moses the Ethiopian or the Black. Cult and representation in the Middle Ages," *Zograf* 43 (2019): 1-22.

[10] Lucien Regnault, *Abbé Isaïe. Recueil ascétique: Introduction et traduction française par les moines des Solesmes*, (Bégrolles: Abbaye de Bellefontaine, 1970). These are not in John

edition of the *Bustān ar-Ruhbān* and comprise *Isaiah 16 (1-11)* and *Isaiah 7: Spiritual Counsels* of this book.[11] The teachings of this text focuses on juxtaposing the practical methods of ascetical living with their spiritual value—similar to Christ's pedagogical method with the Sermon on the Mount. The primary spiritual practice is to keep the fear of God (*al-khawf min Allah*) at the forefront of a monk's habit, drawing one into the deep contemplation of God (*al-hadīd*) and knowledge of God (*ma'rifa*)—these will be discussed later. But his teachings recorded by Abba Isaiah bears similar lessons to that of John Cassian and Germanus' dialogue with Abba Moses in the first two chapters of his *Conferences*.[12]

Many lay people fled to the wilderness seeking the monastic life in this region and eventually composed hymns and wrote icons to

---

Chryssaygis and Pachomios Penkett (translators), *Abba Isaiah of Scetis: Ascetic Discourses* (MI: Cistercian Publications, 2002). For an analysis on the various recensions of the text, see Derwas J. Chitty, "Abba Isaiah," *The Journal of Theological Studies*, Volume XXII, Issue I (Oxford University Press, April 1971): 47–72.
https://doi.org/10.1093/jts/XXII.I.47

[11] Bishop Epiphanius must have believed that this Abba Moses was the same Abba Moses of our book, and hence added these sayings under Moses the Black: *Bustān ar-Ruhbān* (Cairo: St Macarius Monastery, 2014), 101-8.

[12] Wortley indicates that Abba Moses of Scetis and Abba Moses the Black are the same person. See *Give me a word*, 193 n.87. The *Conferences* are lengthy and already widely known to English readers, therefore, they are not inscribed in this book. Beginning to build a framework of Abba Moses's ascetical theology is Jean-Luc Molinier, "Abba Moïse l'Éthiopien, moine de Scété, et sa trajectoire de sanctification," *Collectanea Cisterciensia* 77, no. 4 (2015): 343-367. See also, Paul Devos, "Saint Jean Cassien et saint Moïse l'Éthiopien," *Analecta Bollandiana* 103, no. 1-2 (1985): 61-74.

A Note on the Texts

venerate Abba Moses who drew them to Christ. One can gauge more about how the Coptic Church celebrated and knew Abba Moses by gleaning over the several hymns composed throughout the centuries. There is no doubt that these hymns were written by the monks of *al-Baramūs* which is evident by phrases like, "Hail to you, O lover of your children" in the *Psali Watos (22)*, and "Come, look and marvel, my fathers the monks" in the *Antiphonary* (15). One of these hymns, given the title here "Another Melody,"[13] was seemingly sung in a monastery in Texas known as St. Mary and St. Moses Abbey. The composers added a verse which states, "In Texas and *Baramūs*, brothers, monks, and priests, all saying, 'ⲁⲍⲓⲟⲥ.'" From the hymns included here, only five were originally sung in Coptic (Doxology 1, 2, Psali Adam and Psali Watos, and the Antiphonary) while the remaining hymns were written in Arabic (Melody, Another Melody, and Salutations), evidently observable from their rhythmic nature.

In this book, text which has been inserted are characterized by square brackets. With respect to the Arabic *Sīra*, I have followed Pirone's divisions and have not included the foliation. The subheadings of the divisions are my own. Arabic words are transliterated and applies sun and moon letters (or solar letters) to assimilate the letter *lām* (in 'al') i.e., *Wādī an-Naṭrūn* instead of

---

[13] A title given by *Tasbeha.org* to this melody.

Wādī al-Naṭrūn. The numbering of the apophthegmata is the same system Wortley has adopted primarily in *Give me a Word*. The *sayings* (*aqwāl*) that constitute *Moses 14-17* have been renumbered to follow the remaining apophthegmata. Those from Bishop Epiphanius's edition of the *Bustān* have been translated to English here for the first time.

The hymns which constitute the last section of this book are more or less consistent with the translations that have already been published by the Coptic Reader mobile application. When citing the hymns, the title of the hymn will be italicized followed by the strophe's number. I have amended the translation of some verses where necessary according to its respective tune for rhythm and flow and at times, linguistic accuracy.

CHAPTER ONE
INTRODUCTION

> Who has ever seen a thief who believed in a king as this
> penitent thief who through his faith stole the Kingdom of
> Heaven and the Paradise of joy?
>
> — Hymn of the Penitent Thief[14]

The book you hold in your hands pays homage to one of the most renowned saints of the Coptic Church—Abba Moses the Strong. Many have embraced the biography and counsel of Abba Moses as a relatable mentor of the spiritual life. The reader will not only engage with the life of Abba Moses, but also that which is expressed in ancient literature, hymnography, and iconography.

Abba Moses was born in the year c. AD 332.[15] He is also known by the titles Moses the Robber, Moses the Ethiopian and Moses the Strong. In the Coptic tradition the two titles most common to him are "the Black" and "the Strong." The former title mostly attested to in the Copto-Arabic manuscript tradition of his biography, and the latter is mostly known in Coptic hymnography. There is even an instance where he is given the title "ⲁⲃⲃⲁ ⲙⲱⲥⲏ ⲡⲓⲙⲁⲧⲟⲓ ⲛ̀ϫⲱⲣⲓ

---

[14] 6th Hour of Coptic Great Friday
[15] This date is supported by MS B–M which states he lived up to the age of 75. *Vita di Mosè l'Etiope*, 68.

(Abba Moses, the Mighty Soldier)."[16] But the Coptic parishioner who hears the liturgical biography of the saints (the Synaxarium), will notice the unique exposition by which the compiler decided to conclude the reading; an occurrence that does not appear with any other saint:

> Contemplate, O beloved, the power of repentance and its work. [Repentance] moved an infidel, slave, murderer, adulterer, and a robber, and turned him into a great father, teacher, comforter, and priest who wrote canons for the monks; a saint whose name is remembered on the altar. To this day, his body rests in the Monastery of *al-Baramūs*. May his prayers be with us now and forever. Amen.[17]

Not only were the Coptic hymn composers and biography writers so inspired by him, but his influence extends far beyond the Orthodox tradition. Western churches *unofficially* celebrate this

---

[16] This is found in a hymn which appears in the 15th-century known as ⲉⲅⲭⲉⲥ ([through] the prayers). See Fr ʿAṭṭālla Arsaniyūs al-Muḥarraqī, ⲡϫⲱⲙ ⲛ̀ⲧⲙⲉⲧⲣⲉϥϣⲉⲙϣⲓ ⲛ̀ⲧⲉ ⲡⲓⲇⲓⲁⲕⲱⲛ ⲛⲉⲙ ⲛⲓⲃⲱϩⲉⲙ (Cairo, 1973), 482 – 484; a study of this hymn is published in Arabic by Youhanna Nessim Youssef, *Aḍwāʾ ʿala ar-Rahbana al-Qibṭiyya* (Cairo: Alexandria School, 2018), 103 – 106.

[17] *PO* Tome 17 (1923), 591-4.

saint, adopting lessons from his ascetical struggle and spiritual wisdom.[18]

Sozomen, a renowned Roman lawyer and Church historian, known for his extensive *Ecclesiastical History*[19] dedicated to Emperor Theodosius I (AD 347–395), wrote about Abba Moses roughly 70 years after his martyrdom in c. AD 407. His work collects the history of the Church from AD 323 to AD 425. In Book VI Chapter 29, *On the monks of Thebais*, Sozomen dedicates a small subchapter to Abba Moses. He introduces Moses as "an Egyptian" (ένας Αιγύπτιος). Another Moses is mentioned, but that is Moses the Libyan.[20] The account is a redacted version of that which is found in the *Lausiac History*. Sozomen's account reads:

> About the same time the celebrated Mark, Macarius the younger, Apollonius, and Moses, an Egyptian, dwelt at Scetis....[21]

---

[18] Examples can be found in several western artwork, blogs, and local community flyers. A great source that was recently published is a retelling of Abba Moses's biography for students at a Catholic School, St. Benedicts Academy: Andrew Votipka, *Abba Moses: Notorios Robber, Desert Father* (Bearded Books, 2020).

[19] PG 67, 1377. For an English translation see, Edward Walford, *History of the Church by Sozomen and Philostorgius* (London: John Childs and Son, Bungay, 1855), 291–292.

[20] There are a number of saints who lived within the same period by the name of Moses. Fr. John Paul Abdelsayed (now Bishop Kyrillos, Dean of St. Athanasius and St. Cyril's Coptic Orthodox Theological College in Los Angeles) lists the various saints by the name of Moses: *The Strong Saint Abba Moses* (California: Saint Paul Brotherhood Press, 2010), 16–19.

[21] PG 67, 1377. For an English translation, see *History of the Church by Sozomen and Philostorgius*, trans. E. Walford (London 1855), 291–292.

Arsenius 38 also testifies to Moses' Egyptian ethnicity. Palladius of Galatia (363–420s), at the request of Lausus, chamberlain at the court of the Byzantine Emperor Theodosius II, wrote the *Lausiac History,* which is an influential work that captures, in short insertions, the lives of the Desert Fathers. This, however, presents Moses as an Ethiopian, which happens to be his most attributed nationality. In the Coptic text of Palladius, he is given the name ⲘⲞⲨⲤⲎ ⲠⲒⲬⲀⲘⲎ (Moses the Black).[22] It seems that this text has found favor in later hagiography (writing the lives of saints) and was expanded on by various traditions, such as the Copto-Arabic tradition attested to in our book. Palladius's version includes the subchapter "Moses the Robber," a title that was not used much in later Copto-Arabic texts. At some stage, this *History*[23] was translated to Coptic, first to Sahidic, then to the Bohairic dialect, but

---

[22] Emile Amélineau, *De Historia Lausiaca quaenam sit hujus ad monachorum aegyptiorum historiam scribendam utilitas: adjecta sunt quaedam hujus Historiae coptica fragmenta inedita* (E. Leroux, 1887), 262. Gabra also identifies this title ⲘⲞⲨⲤⲎ ⲠⲒⲬⲒⲘⲀ, and says it is sometimes simultaneous with ⲈⲐⲰϢ (Nubian or Ethiopian) see Gabra, "Bemerkungen zu Moses dem Schwartzen," 125. See also the definition and analysis in Walter E. Crum, *A Coptic Dictionary* (Oxford: Clarendon Press, 1939), 110. For the relationship between Palladius' *Historia Lausiaca* and the Coptic texts, see Gabriel Bunge, "Palladiana: I. Introduction aux fragments coptes de l'Histoire Lausiaque," *Studia Monastica* 32 (1990): 79–129.

[23] O'Leary De Lacy, *The saints of Egypt in the Coptic calendar* (London – New York 1937), 31; Gawdat Gabra, "Bemerkungen zu Moses dem Schwartzen," in ΘΕΜΕΛΙΑ: *Spätantike und koptologische Studien Peter Grossmann zum 65, Geburstag,* ed. M. Krause, S. Schaten, (Wiesbaden, 1998): 118; De Lacy O'Leary, *The Difnar (Antiphonarium) of the Coptic Church,* Vol. 3: *Bashons, Baounah, Abib, Mesre and the intercalary days or Nasi* (London, 1930), 22.

unfortunately only fragments from the 10th century survive.[24] The rubrics that appear from the *Life of Abba Pambo* in this text suggests that it may have had a liturgical function.[25]

Another important text to consider is the *Alphabetical Collection of The Sayings of the Desert Fathers*, known as the *Apophthegmata Patrum* compiled in the fifth or sixth century.[26] In the Christian Arabic tradition, this work is known as *Bustān ar-Ruhbān* (lit. the garden of the monks) or commonly referred to in English as the *Paradise of the Fathers*. In it, there is a chapter on Abba Moses titled, "concerning Abba Moses." The events of his life prior to monasticism are not included and the text focuses on short lessons concerning his struggle against *logismoi* and *porneia* as well as his conversations with Abba Isidore.[27] Of course, the purpose for compiling the *Apophthegmata* was not to provide a history of any Desert Father, rather it was to be a pedagogy of spiritual wisdom for the monks. It is a text which has become part of the prescribed canon of readings for monks along with Scripture and the horologion. The

---

[24] Emile Amélineau completed an edition to this text in *De Historia Lausiaca quaenam sit hujus ad monachorum aegyptiorum historiam scribendam utilitas: adjecta sunt quaedam hujus Historiae coptica fragmenta inedita* (E. Leroux, 1887), 73-124.

[25] The rubric: "The fifth Sunday of Lent." See Edward Cuthbert Butler (ed.), *The Lausiac history of Palladius I. A critical discussion together with notes on early Egyptian monachism*, 111.

[26] Youssef, *Aḍwā ʿala ar-Rahbana al-Qibṭiyya*, 17 – 18.

[27] *PG* 65, 281–289. For the English translation, see Benedicta Ward (trans.), *The sayings of the desert fathers: the alphabetical collection*, (Kentucky: Cistercian Publishing, 1975), 138–143. The edition of the sayings I have relied on is that of John Wortley, trans., *Give Me a Word: The Alphabetical Sayings of the Desert Fathers* (New York: St. Vladimir's Seminary Press, 2014).

text of the *Apophthegmata* survives in Sahidic and was first published almost two centuries ago![28] Gabra notes that this text may have been the foundation of the Arabic *Sīra* by providing a parallel comparison of both the Coptic and Arabic texts to display its word-for-word translation.[29]

The hymnography is an important derivative of the above texts that infused into the liturgical life of the Church. The earliest extant hymns in honor of Abba Moses, to my knowledge, seem to be the Bohairic Antiphonarium. One would think that there must have been a hymn composed in Sahidic for Abba Moses, but I did not find this in the Sahidic Antiphonarium recently published by the Coptic scholar, Mr. Mickel Helmy.[30] Gabra published the text of the Bohairic Antiphonary relying on a manuscript from the Monastery of St. Antony in the Red Sea, Egypt, after finding that the edition by O'Leary was lacking in some parts.[31] Hymns add, and at times emphasize, important details about a saint that are not particularly known through other sources. For example, the Melodies include a story of an angel that appears when Abba Moses confesses to Abba

---

[28] The Coptic text is found in Georgio Zoega, *Catalogus codicum Copticorum manu scriptorum qui in Museo Borgiano Velitris adservantur* (Roma, 1810), 318. It was later republished by Marius Chaîne, *Le Manuscrit de la version copte en dialecte sahidique des "Apophthegmata Patrum"* (Le Caire: Impr. de l'Institut français d'archéologie orientale, 1960), 45–46.

[29] Gabra, "Bemerkungen zu Moses dem Schwartzen," 108–120.

[30] Mickel Helmy, ed., *ad-Difnār: al-Antīfūnāriyūn aṣ-Ṣaʿīdī* (Cairo: Alexandria School, 2018).

[31] Gabra, "Bemerkungen zu Moses dem Schwartzen," 121–124.

Macarius, and with each confession, the angel wipes away the sins written on the tablet (Melody #14).

However, it was the text of Palladius which became the framework of various traditions which expounded on his version. The Arabic version pays particular attention to that of the *Lausiac History* and aims at tailoring the biography to a monastic community. The use of words such as "*abānā*" or "*abūna*" (our father) to dictate the story is already enough evidence to suggest that the audience has shifted from Palladius's commoner to the monks of Egypt. More specific terms like "*al-ekhwa*" (the brethren) or "*ar-ruhbān*" (the monks) places those who are listening to or reciting the story as among those discipled by Abba Moses. The same can be said about the hymns which ask for the saint to bless the "assembly" of the monks.

We know that a community of monks formed in the region in which Abba Moses dwelled even before he entered the desert. Sts. Maximus and Dometius departed in the year 384, and shortly after their departure, there began the growth of a monastic community, eventually leading to the construction of *al-Baramūs*, a monastery in their namesake.[32] There are two monasteries by this name: the Old *Baramūs*, which is the original monastery now in ruins, and the

---

[32] The four saints (Sts. Maximus and Dometius, Isidore, and Moses) were either from the same monastic lavra or very close to each other.

Modern *Baramūs* which was constructed as a counterpart monastery.[33] It is widely known that this monastery was named after the Virgin Mary in honor of the siblings Maximus and Dometius,[34] but the monastery began to be identified with Abba Moses from about the 9th century (possibly earlier).[35] According to the 11th century list of monasteries compiled by Deacon Mawhūb ibn Manṣūr ibn Mufarrij al-Iskandarānī in the *History of the Patriarchs*, there were seven monasteries in Wādī an-Naṭrūn, one of which was *Dayr Anba Mūsa al-Aswad* (the Monastery of Abba Moses the Black).[36] This same text tells a story of the Abbot from the Monastery of John Kame who threatens to leave his monastery and retire to the "Caves of Abba Moses" should any of the archons coming from Cairo visit him. At that time, Mawhūb identified twenty monks living in *al-Baramūs* and two monks in the Cave of Moses. Evelyn White suggests that this monastery "must have been small and remote."[37] Our 14th-century *Sīra* identifies the monastery

---

[33] The modern Monastery of *al-Baramūs* that was founded next to the old Baramūs as a "twin monastery" was in fact established in the 6th century as a result of a theological controversy between Julian, bishop Halicarnassus (†518) and St. Severus, Patriarch of Antioch (†ca. 465–583) on the corruptibility or incorruptibility of Christ before the resurrection. See, Gawdat Gabra, *Coptic Monasteries: Egypt's Monastic Art and Architecture* (Oxford University Press, 2002), 38–42.

[34] For the construction and naming of this monastery, see Nessim, *The Life of Sts Maximus and Dometius*, 71–77.

[35] Youssef, *Aḍwā ʿala ar-Rahbana al-Qibṭiyya*, 103–106.

[36] *History of the Patriarchs*, 645.

[37] Evelyn White, *The Monasteries of the Wâdi'n Natrûn vol. II the History of the Monasteries of Nitria and Scetis*, 303–304.

of *al-Baramūs* to be the place which was named after him (§21). Only a century later, this monastery was ruined and left unoccupied.[38] MS G adds an interesting point about this monastery and states:

> Many brothers came to [Abba Moses] and begged to dwell with him. They were growing day by day until they became five hundred in number. The four monasteries became prosperous on the Mountain of Scetis. This monastery of Abba Moses is called *al-Baramūs*. Abba Isidore the priest built the first church there. The other which is next to it is known as the Church of Abba Pishoi and the other below it is known as the Church of Abba John, and the other is the Church of Abba Macarius the Great.
>
> When Abba Moses became a priest, he built a new church in a place known to this day as the Church of Abba Moses.[39]

By some means, the monastery became incorrectly identified with Abba Moses. White suggests that there may have been a confusion due to a false etymology in the Arabic term "*Baramūs*" for Abba Mūsa. However, I wish to elaborate that the muddle is more likely to do with the Arabic wording "*al-Bār Mūsa*", (or *al-Bār Mūsi* if one were to read the name with *yeh* instead of *alif maqṣūra*) which translates to "the righteous, Moses." This is evident several times in

---

[38] Fr. Ṣamū'īl Ṭāwaḍrūs as-Suryānī, *al-ʾAdyūra al-Maṣriya al-ʿAmera*, 183.
[39] *Vita di Mosè l'Etiope*, 95–96.

MS B–M, where the scribe switches been "*al-Bār Mūsa*" and *"Mūsa al-Bār."*[40]

Fr. Ṣamū'īl Ṭāwaḍrūs as-Suryānī noted in one of the manuscripts of the Patriarchate containing the ritual of the Holy Myron that Pope Benjamin II, after completing the concoction in the Monastery of St. Macarius in the year 1330, travelled to "the monastery of our Roman Fathers which is known as *al-Baramūs*, entered the holy church and prostrated before the altar. He took the blessings of the honorable relics and of the pure body of St. Abba Moses." [41]

Many sources indicate Petra[42] to be the place of his retirement. This so-called Petra, also known as the "The Rock of Macarius" is likely to be the same place of the so-called monastery of Abba Moses (cf. *Psali Watos* 6) which was a cave or small church located near the Old *Baramūs,* or some fifty meters from the present-day monastery,[43] as attested to in *Doxology 1.5*. At some stage, and implied in the *Psali Adam 2*, the relics were relocated to the Modern

---

[40] At first glance, one reading the text would think that the scribe is referring to Abba Moses using the byname "*al-Baramūsī*," often given to men who are tonsured at this monastery. See *Vita di Mosè l'Etiope*, 55–70.

[41] Fr. Ṣamū'īl Ṭāwaḍrūs as-Suryānī, *al-ʿAdyūra al-Maṣriya al-ʿAmera*, 184.

[42] From the Coptic ⲡⲉⲧⲣⲁ meaning "rock."

[43] Karel C. Innemee, "Deir al-Baramūs, excavations at the so-called site of Moses the Black, 1994-1999" *BSAC* 39 (2000): 123–135; Karel C. Innemme, "Excavations at the site of Deir Al-Baramūs 2002-2005" *BSAC* 44 (2005): 55–68. On Petra, see the theories presented by White, *The Monasteries of the Wâdi'n Natrûn vol. II*, 422 and 447–448; "Jabal Khashm Al-Qu'ud" in *CE*: https://ccdl.claremont.edu/digital/collection/cce/id/1059/rec/1

Baramūs possibly during the 11th century raid that threatened the monastic establishments in Wādī an-Naṭrūn.

CHAPTER TWO
THE TIMES OF ABBA MOSES

> A believer is not one who thinks that God can do everything, but one who believes that he will obtain all things. Faith paves the way for what seems impossible; and the right-hand thief proved this for himself.
>
> — St John Climacus[44]

Abba Moses lived at a time where desert monasticism in the Wilderness of Scetis had begun to thrive under the spiritual direction of Abba Macarius the Great (AD 300–391). By this time, the Edict of Milan (AD 313) had already taken effect for at least 15 years, and Christianity began one of its most influential phases of Church history: the birth of desert spirituality.

To place the context in which Abba Moses lived, we should consider the era of martyrdom that plagued Christians leading up to his birth in AD 332 since during that time, the wilderness became a place to flee persecution.

In Egypt more specifically, and at least for the first two hundred years, persecution was sporadic, until the Severan persecution in AD 202. Much is not known about that period. It is during the time of

---

[44] John Climacus, *The Ladder of Divine Ascent*, Step 26.68.

Pope Dionysius of Alexandria (+265), who was enthroned one year before the beginning of the Decian persecution, that we begin to learn about mass persecution. In AD 250, Emperor Decius releases an edict that all citizens of the Roman Empire must sacrifice to the gods. Certificates (*libelli*) to those who sacrificed were issued. At about the same period, St Jerome (c. AD 347–420) tells us about St. Paul the Hermit (AD 227–341) fleeing into the desert because of the persecution.[45] St Jerome described the persecution writing,

> Many churches in Egypt and the Thebaid were laid waste by the fury of the storm. At that time the Christians would often pray that they might be smitten with the sword for the name of Christ. But the desire of the crafty foe was to slay the soul, not the body; and this he did by searching diligently for slow but deadly tortures.[46]

Many were martyred, and more were tortured and imprisoned. Several renounced their faith because of the severity of the tortures, but others had not, and still lived, becoming what the Church terms

---

[45] Jerome states, "The young man had the tact to understand this, and, conforming his will to the necessity, fled to the mountain wilds to wait for the end of the persecution" (Jerome, "The Life of Paulus the First Hermit," in NPNF² 6, 299–303). See also al-Qiddīs Ǧīrūm, *Ṯhlāṯh Siyyar Biqalam al-Qiddīs Ǧīrūm: al-Anbā Būlā Awal al-Sawāḥ, al-Qiddīs Hīlāriyūn, al-Qiddīs Malkḫūs al-Rāhib al-Asīr*, Fr Yūḥanā ʿAṭā Maḥrūs (trans.), (Cairo: Alexandria School, 2019), s. 5. Dr Lisa Agaiby is currently leading an academic work on the Life of St. Paul the Hermit which tackles eight ancient traditions of the biography.

[46] Jerome, "The Life of Paulus the First Hermit," in NPNF² 6, 299–303.

"confessors."⁴⁷ They healed, pardoned sins, and converted many people who would visit them in prison. Pope Dionysius (+265) had also fled the persecution by the providence of God, while remaining visible to his community through his written homilies and letters aimed at affirming the faith of the believers and addressing their doubts. Amid the persecutions, Pope Dionysius beautifully wrote:

> But we did not abstain even from the visible assembling of ourselves together in the Lord's presence, but those who were in the city [Alexandria] I the more earnestly urged to assemble, as if I were still with them, being absent in the body, as it says, but present in the spirit. And at Cephro also a large number of the Church were sojourning with us, consisting of the brethren who had followed us from the city or were present from other parts of Egypt. There, too, the Lord opened us a door for the word. And at first, we were pursued and stoned, but later not a few of the Gentiles left their idols and turned to God. Thus, the word was first sown through us in their hearts who had not previously received it. And as it were for this cause God having led us to them, led us away again when we had fulfilled this ministry.⁴⁸

Between the Decian and the Diocletianic persecutions, there was a small window of about fifty-two years where persecution became

---

[47] Archbishop Basilios, "Martyrdom" in CE:
https://ccdl.claremont.edu/digital/collection/cce/id/1288/rec/15

[48] *St. Dionysius of Alexandria: Letters and Treatises*, Charles Lett Feltoe (trans.), (London – New York: The Macmillan Company, 1918), 46-47.

sporadic again. When Diocletian had begun his rule in AD 284, he did not instantly seek to wipe out Egyptian Christians because they were already oppressed and not yet considered a threat to him. During this time of minor relief, Pope Peter of Alexandria I (+311) was enthroned.

Diocletian's reign was largely one for expansion and dominance. The conflict between himself and the Christians was rather triggered when he attempted to deify himself, not just as the "son of god," as other Emperors had, but as "god."[49] Egyptian Christians were among the first to contest his public demonstrations by signing themselves with the cross. Diocletian, now seeing Christians as a threat to his deification, releases an edict in 303 for the burning of scriptures, demolition of Churches, and stripping Christians and clergy of their social ranks. Eusebius, the Church historian, recorded this event and wrote:

> 23 Feb. It was in the nineteenth year of the reign of Diocletian, (302-303) in the month of March, when the feast of the Savior's passion was near at hand, that royal edicts were published everywhere, commanding that the churches be levelled to the ground and the scriptures be destroyed by fire, and ordering that those who held places of honor be degraded, and that the

---

[49] Richard Valantasis, Douglas K. Bleyle, and Dennis C. Haugh, *The Gospels and Christian Life in History and Practice* (Maryland: Rowman & Littlefield Publishers, 2009), 189.

household servants, if they persisted in the profession of Christianity, be made slaves.[50]

Spring/Summer. Such was not the first edict against us. But not long after, other decrees were issued, commanding that all the rulers of the churches in every place be first thrown into prison, and afterwards be compelled to sacrifice by whatever means necessary.[51]

Torture became an authorized form of punishment. Clergy were arrested and compelled to sacrifice to pagan gods. Tradition tells us that the tortures were so great, that the blood of the martyrs was like a pool reaching the knees of a horse in height.[52] No doubt, there were monastics like Abba Antony and his disciples who lived during this period but spent much of their time away from persecution. Their warfare, as St. Paul says, was "against the rulers, authorities, cosmic powers over this present darkness, and against the spiritual forces of evil in the heavenly places" (Ephesians 6:12). But even Abba Antony himself would come down from the mountain to seek martyrdom and would instead, as God willed for him, comfort and minister to those who were persecuted. The image we have of Antony is not just someone who lived in seclusion—indeed, this is true—but he was

---

[50] Eusebius, *Historia Ecclesiastica*, 8.4.
[51] Ibid, 8.2.5.
[52] See Alan K. Bowman, *Egypt after the Pharaohs, 332 BC-AD 642: from Alexander to the Arab Conquest* (Oakland, CA: University of California Press, 1996), 45.

also a present father for those in persecution. St. Athanasius (†373) describes:

> Afterwards, the persecution of Maximin came upon the Church, and when the holy martyrs were led into Alexandria, Antony left his monastic dwelling and followed them, saying, "let us also go and face the contest with the holy ones if we are called, or witness those who fight." For he wanted to be a martyr and remained to minister to the confessors in the mines and prisons. He demonstrated great determination on behalf of those who had been called before the law courts to face the contest and trained them to be steadfast. He would kiss and embrace those who were going to be martyrs, walking with them until they were perfected.[53]

Martyrdom and monasticism were not distant concepts. Some have often referred to the monk as an extension of the martyr, or a spiritual martyr. We know that their roles intertwined, co-existed, and influenced each other. During this era of persecution, the role of the monk was pivotal in reviving faith to the lay community because they served as spiritual fathers to those who had lost family members, homes, and livelihoods.

When Pope Peter I (†311) was enthroned on the See of St. Mark, he was also forced to flee. While Pope Peter was away, he remained vigilant in his pastoral ministry by sending letters that the clergy

---

[53] Vivian and Athanassakis, *The Life of Antony*, 156.

would read out to comfort the people. There was a small period of time between AD 305–306 where he returned to Alexandria. To make the most of this period, Pope Peter I wrote his famous canonical letters which addressed issues around those who had left the faith because of persecution, and the penance required of them to return. He was very understanding and accepting of everyone's circumstances and received many of the lapsed Christians into communion. What is interesting to note is that the Coptic Church adopted the era of martyrs not by the death of Diocletian, but by the martyrdom of Peter i.e., "the seal of the martyrs." In a lengthy martyrdom story written in Coptic, there is a scene where Peter is taken to the tomb of St. Mark to face his death. As he kisses the tomb a lady experiences a vision where she hears the words, "Peter was the first of the apostles, now he is the last of the martyrs!"[54] During this period of martyrdom, many began to bear witness to the wisdom and deep spirituality that was springing from the desert. This is especially true when considering that these ascetics were not so distant from those being martyred, as per the example of Abba Antony, being well aware of the martyrdoms occurring around them.[55] In fact people tried to escape this era of persecution by fleeing to the monasteries, they were not freed from the hands of the

---

[54] *ABC*, 61 (N. 69).
[55] Some of these examples can be found in *More Anons.*, 37 (N.41), 39 (N.42), 375-378 (N. 551).

berbers who raided and looted monasteries, often slaughtering the monks.

Abba John Colobus, a contemporary who lived nearby Abba Moses, shares a parallel account to the martyrdom of Abba Moses but in his case, justifiably flees with the brethren:

> Many days after he returned from Alexandria, the berbers ruled Scetis with tyrannical and despicable deeds, it was said, destroying the peace, tranquility, and way of life of our fathers with their animalistic ways, threatening the monks and destroying the holy places. As our father was making haste to leave Scetis, it is said that all the brothers tearfully surrounded him, saying to him, "Will you also leave, our father? Are you afraid of the berbers?" Our holy father Abba John answered them, "By the name of Christ God, I am not afraid. No, the perfect goodness in God's presence does not allow each of us to pursue his own salvation alone; instead, according to an angelic purpose, each of us, especially the devout person, performs all his deeds while regarding his own good and that of his brother equally. This barbarian, even if he is separated from me by faith, nevertheless is an image and creature of God in the same way that I am. If I resist this barbarian, he will kill me and

will go to punishment because of me." And with these words he left Scetis.[56]

Now that the transition between the era of martyrdom and monasticism was not so much two separate stages, rather the fruit of one tree, the Egyptian desert had slowly become the place where the *martyrs without shedding blood* travelled. The monks themselves began to acknowledge this new form of martyrdom when they spoke about the monastic life. Abba Macarius, when he was telling the story of *two strangers* (Sts. Maximus and Dometius), concludes with the words, "Come, see the martyrs' shrine of the young strangers"[57]—though they were not physically martyred! Another example comes from an *apophthegm* of Abba Pambo:

> Four monks of Scetis, clothed in skins, came one day to see the great Pambo. Each one revealed the virtue of his neighbor. The first fasted a great deal; the second was poor; the third had acquired great charity; and they said of the fourth that he had lived for twenty-two years in obedience to an elder. Abba Pambo said to them, "I tell you, the virtue of this last one is the greatest. Each of the others has obtained the virtue he wished to acquire; but the last one, restraining his own will, does the will of another. **Now it**

---

[56] For the Coptic text, see Émile Amélineau, *Histoire des monastères de la Basse-Egypte: vies des Saints Paul, Antoine, Macaire, Maxime et Domèce Jean le Nain.* vol. 25 (Paris: Leroux, 1894), 316-413. The English translation here is from Maged S. Mikhail and Tim Vivian, "Zacharias of Sakha: An Encomium on the Life of John the Little," *Coptic Church Review* 18, no 1-2 (1997): 1-64.
[57] *Give me a word*, Macarius the Egyptian 33, 190.

is of such men that the martyrs are made, if they persevere to the end." [58]

Abba Pambo refers to the vow of obedience that a monk is required to take, and it is by this that the spiritual martyr (a monk) is formed. The martyrdom they sought was one that constituted tears of *metanoia*:

> [An elder said]: "I believe that God counts a man who of his own free will hands himself over to affliction as one of the martyrs, for instead of blood, tears are counted to his credit."[59]

The words of the Patriarch Athanasius (†373) who himself encouraged people to "suffer martyrdom in their conscience; die to sin"[60] echoes the spiritual martyrdom of the monastic. He advised the faithful community not to wage war with emperors and rulers but follows the words of the Apostle Paul that the warfare is indeed a spiritual one (cf. Eph. 6:10-20). Lay men and women sought a philosophy of life that deepened the meaning of their existence by continual prayer and training in virtue. This holy lifestyle aimed to bring the monk into a state of spiritual communion with God through various ascetical means. Monks are often termed "angels on earth," since they commit to the work of the angels—i.e., unceasing praises. In antiquity, this took dedication and patient endurance—

---

[58] I have chosen to use the translation given by Ward: *The Sayings of the Desert Fathers*, 196.
[59] *More Anons.*, 369 (N.539).
[60] Ibid, 481-483 (N.600).

"not [to be] sub-human but super-human" by means of very human activities.[61] The young and ambitious monk, Abba John Colobos, believing he can transcend manual labor, said to his elder brother:

> I wanted to be free of concern just as the angels are free of concern, not working at all, but unceasingly worshipping God.[62]

This idea is mirrored by the hymnography composed to commemorate the saints. However, their image is much more than people who spent their life in "unceasing praise." One might even argue that unceasing praise is more than just chanting or recitation. It is a combination of *hesychia*—the act of bringing oneself to stillness and tranquility—and *metanoia*—the act of continually remembering one's sins, combined with prostrations.

For desert monastics, unceasing prayer would lead them to grow in Christ-like fervor and virtue. The example of Abba Antony is very telling of the monastic's pursuit for virtue. The first statement that introduces his *Life* reads:

> You have entered a good contest with the monks of Egypt, having determined in your heart to make yourselves their equal or to surpass them in the virtue of your ascetic discipline.[63]

---

[61] Ward, *The Sayings of the Desert Fathers*, xxiii.

[62] *Give me a word*, John Colobos 2, 131.

[63] Based on the Coptic translation in Tim Vivian and Apostolos Athanassakis (trans.), *The Life of Antony: The Coptic Life and Greek Life* (MI: Cistercian Publications, 2003), 50.

Chapter Two: The Times of Abba Moses

"Virtue" appears about twenty times in Athanasius's *Life of Antony*. The more one chased virtue, the more one became active in the divine life—the life *in* Christ. Such was the case of Abba Moses. MS B–M stresses his virtuous life by stating:

> The righteous (Moses) remained in his cell observing silence. He would try to hide his virtue as much as he could and would not seek the praise of men. He loved humility and meekness, but his virtue became known to many people—to the same extent of fame as his previous miserable and villainous life. He eventually became an anchorite adorned with virtue. As the apostle Paul said, "Where sin abounded, grace abounded all the more." [Rom. 5:20][64]

However, the journey toward virtue for any saint was not easy. The elders often spoke about the importance of virtue and that attaining it came through "hard work"[65] and "tears."[66] Abba Antony, being the father of monasticism and "trainer for those who run well,"[67] was the

---

[64] *Vita di Mosè l'Etiope*, 60.

[65] "Somebody said to the blessed Arsenius: 'How is it that we have gained nothing from so much education and wisdom, while these rustic Egyptian peasants have acquired such virtues?' Abba Arsenius said to him: 'For our part we have gained nothing from the world's education, but these rustic Egyptian peasants have acquired the virtues by their own labours.'" *Give me a word*, Abba Arsenius 5, 41.

[66] "A brother asked Abba Poemen: 'What am I to do about my sins?' The elder said to him: 'One who wishes to redeem his sins redeems them by weeping, and he who wishes to acquire virtues acquires them by weeping. Weeping is the way scripture and our fathers passed down to us, saying 'Weep! For there is no other way but that one'" [cf. Jas 4:9]. Ibid, Abba Poemen 118, 248.

[67] From Tone 6 of the Great Vespers of Abba Antony in the Byzantine tradition. See Marguerite Pazis (ed.), *Festal Vespers Hymns: 17 January, St Anthony the Great, Holy Heiromartyr and*

architype of the practical manner by which a monk learns to struggle toward virtuousness.

It is in this period, whereby Abba Antony is now discipling monks, that we are introduced to Abba Macarius the Great (AD 300–390) who journeyed into the Libyan desert for a life of solitude at AD 330, two years before Abba Moses was born. Before establishing the famous Wilderness of Scetis, Abba Macarius himself needed discipleship, and so he visited Abba Antony twice; once in AD 343 and a second time in AD 352. Abba Antony encouraged him and addressed his spiritual warfare saying, "from these hands (Macarius') much strength comes out!"[68] Abba Antony after having instructed him on monastic life and on how to tackle *logismoi*, gave him the monastic habit and the mantle.[69] Fatherhood was conferred on Abba Macarius by the symbol of the mantle; he would become a figure of spiritual nourishment for the region of *Wādī an-Naṭrūn*. And it was after this second visit (AD 352) that churches would be built in monastic establishments. Many monks began to form around him because of his *golden mouth* and radiant character. Monasticism developed into a form of semi-anchoritism there. Hermits lived in

---

Founder of Monasticism (Greek Orthodox Patriarchate of Alexandria and all Africa, 29 December 2018), 5. The hymn was written by 6th-century Byzantine saint, Theodore the Sykeote, Bishop of Anastasiopolis.

[68] Tim Vivian (ed.), *St. Macarius the Spirit-bearer: Coptic Texts Relating to Saint Macarius the Great* (New York: St. Vladimir's Seminary Press, 2004), 4.

[69] *St. Macarius the Spirit-bearer*, 177.

self-dug cells or caves that had two or more rooms. A new monk, often called 'brother' discipled himself under an elder to receive spiritual direction and instruction.[70]

In AD 360, Abba Macarius moved further south to the area where the monastery bearing his name now stands, leaving his disciple Abba Paphnutius to carry out his legacy for the community.[71] At this time appears a companion of Abba Macarius, Abba Isidore the Priest,[72] who was one of the abbots of the monastic communities in Scetis before Paphnutius.[73] Meanwhile, we read about Abba Moses venturing out to the wilderness. An interesting statement by Abba Poemen, supposedly after Abba Moses's martyrdom, reads, "Since Abba Moses and the third generation in Scetis, the brothers do not make progress anymore" (Poemen 165). The first generation was that of Abba Macarius, the second, Abba Isidore, and the third was Abba Moses.

---

[70] Gabra, *Coptic Monasteries: Egypt's Monastic Art and Architecture*, 65-6.

[71] Tim Vivian, *St Macarius the Spirit Bearer* (New York: St Vladimir's Seminary Press, 2004), 64, 131, 140, 195.

[72] The *Life of Sts Maximus and Dometius* (St Shenouda Press, 2022), 17, points out that Abba Isidore was a deacon.

[73] *Conferences*, Chapter 15.

CHAPTER THREE
WHO WAS ABBA MOSES?

> He who asks God for less than his desert will certainly
> receive more than he deserves. This is demonstrated by
> the publican who asked for forgiveness but received
> justification. And the robber only asked to be
> remembered in His Kingdom, but he inherited all
> Paradise.
>
> — St John Climacus[74]

In the study of Christian hagiography, there is often an emphasis to read, (and for the scribe, to write) the lives of the monastic fathers in light of Christ's own ministry. For example, in the *Life of Antony*, he heals the ailments of the sick, casts out evil spirits, endures Satan's temptations, and offers counsel to all those who were around him. Athanasius (†373) intentionally presents Antony as an imitator of Christ, a mirror of Christ's ministry—from his miracles to his passion, and into glory. We know that this method of writing biographies was particularly common in many late antique and medieval hagiographical literature. But the *Sīra* of Abba Moses does not bear that same semblance. Nothing is known about his childhood, nor his family. The accounts do not tell us of how he was

---

[74] John Climacus, *The Ladder of Divine Ascent*, Step 24.56.

born of "noble parents" or had a "righteous upbringing." On the contrary, the *Sīra* really emphasizes the portrayal of his ascetical struggle. That is not to say that at times he is not seen to imitate Christ. Indeed, the *sayings* certainly depict him as bearing holy wisdom through his teachings on love and humility. However, I may dare say that his life stands out more than the known "wonder-working" saints because of the constant witness to his struggle above anything else. In fact, it is his own repentance that was *wonder-working*. This contrasts, for instance, the *Life of Sts Maximus and Dometius,* which presents two monastic fathers as virtuous from childhood, who do not seem to have endured much of a battle against their passions per se.[75] From the onset, their biographer praises them for their journey into the monastic life. But this is not the case with Abba Moses. Therefore, it is appropriate that we should reflect on the life of Abba Moses because his struggle really mirrors our own.

The story of Abba Moses begins with his previous life as a robber. One who thinks about this line of business is drawn to believe that robbers are those who steal from others—the definition of a thief. The problem, however, is not with the title "robber," rather that this work was described at a time prior to our own modern definition. "Robber" is from the Greek word λησΤής (*lèstèis*). It is the same word

---

[75] The reader can refer to my previous publication: *The Life of Sts. Maximus and Dometius: Monastery, Hymnography and Iconography* (St. Shenouda Monastery Press, 2022).

St. John the Evangelist uses to describe Barabbas (John 18:40), although he was also an insurrectionist and murderer (Mark 15:7). According to tradition, the right-hand penitent thief who was crucified with Christ was also a notorious murderer;[76] the same of whom Abba Moses identifies himself with in his soliloquy (§5).

Abba Moses was not just an infamous thief. The first story we are told about him concerns his malicious intent to murder a shepherd. When he failed, he went after the sheep, slayed, and skinned them, purchased alcohol, and binged in gluttony and drunkenness (§4). The *Lausiac History* states, "For he was said to go even the length of murder,"[77] and in MS G, "And they used to say that even murder had never bothered him."[78] Even Abba Moses alludes to his murderous past during his own martyrdom when he quotes Christ, "Whoever kills with the sword will be killed by the sword" (Matt. 26:52).[79]

---

[76] This tradition appears in the works of John Chrysostom: "Now, therefore, also, let us approach Him. Rahab was a harlot, yet she was saved; and the thief was a murderer, but he became a citizen of paradise; and Judas, being in the society of the Master, was lost, whilst the thief on the cross became a disciple. These are God's paradoxes. Thus, it was that the Magi found favour, that a publican became an evangelist, and a blasphemer an apostle." Mary H. Allies (trans.), *Leaves from St. John Chrysostom* (South Carolina: BiblioBazaar, 2009), 32.

[77] *Lausiac History*, 87.

[78] *Vita di Mosè l'Etiope*, 81.

[79] §29 of the Arabic *Life*; Moses 10 in the *Sayings*; and the *Antiphonary*. Cf. Gen. 9:6; Exod. 21:12; Rev. 13:10.

Chapter Three: Who Was Abba Moses

One manuscript from the early 18th century at the Red Sea Monastery of St. Paul, Egypt, describes Abba Moses as satanic in the incipit:

> We begin by the help of God Almighty to write the *Sīra* and virtues of [our] father, the great saint, Abba Moses the Black, martyr of our Lord Jesus Christ. It was he who first delivered himself up to Satan and performed several of his commands. At last, he repented and delivered himself up to devotions and [the attainment] of many virtues ...[80]

Thievery, bullying, drunkenness, intimidation, and murder are all the qualities of a robber in antiquity, and a thug in modernity.

Indeed, Abba Moses lived much of his life as a thug. His build, demeanor, and character led many to fear him. One description we have of him comes from the 14th-century *Sīra* presented here, whereby an archon hears about Abba Moses and travels to the desert to meet him. He unknowingly meets Abba Moses who tells the archon not to look for him. When explaining the story to the brethren, the archon describes the man (Abba Moses) as, "... an elderly and saintly man on the road, wearing shabby and filthy clothing..." (§28). In the same story as the one previously mentioned, MS B–M records the archon's words, "[He is] short, his face and body was black, and his hair was white. He was wearing

---

[80] MS St. Paul's Monastery (Hist.) 38, ff. 105v.

rough wool."[81] Another description has him as "a tall black elder wearing rags (*ḥalaqān*)."[82] Consistent with these descriptions is the 13th-century wall painting of Abba Moses at St. Antony's Monastery (figure 1). His appearance, more specifically his skin color, was even used to teach spiritual lessons intended to describe his inner spiritual state.[83] In MS B–M, the prologue introduces the *whiteness* of Abba Moses the Black stating:

> Know that it is impossible for one who is black and Ethiopian to become white. And it is difficult for us to sing praises of Moses, the one who was outwardly and naturally a black Ethiopian, but whose soul eventually became bright and extremely illuminated.[84]

---

[81] *Vita di Mosè l'Etiope*, 61.

[82] An undated manuscript classified Arab 114 in the State and University Library in Göttingen. See Hrsg. von Wilhelm Meyer. Bd. 3: Universitätsbibliothek. Nachlässe von Gelehrten, Orientalische Handschriften. Handschriften im Besitz von Instituten und Behörden. Register zu Band 1 - 3. Berlin: Bath, 1894. (Verzeichniss der Handschriften im preußischen Staate 1, Hannover, 3), 371-372. Gawdat Gabra pointed out that the same version was also found in a manuscript housed in the library of *Dayr al-Suryān* under no. 308, which dates from 1314. Cf. Gawdat Gabra, "Dair Anba Musa al-Aswad: das originale Baramus Kloster in Wadi al-Natrun", *BSAC* 36 (1997) 72–73.

[83] Some scholars have commented on his skin color in his biography and sayings: David Brakke, *Demons and the making of the monk: spiritual combat in early Christianity* (Harvard University Press, 2009), 179-80; O'Brien Wicker K, "Ethiopian Moses" (collected sources), *Ascetic behavior in Greco-Roman antiquity*, ed., V. L. Wimbush (Minneapolis 1990): 329–348; Brian Noell, "Race in Late Antique Egypt: Moses the Black and Authentic Historical Voice", Eras 6 (2004). https://www.monash.edu/arts/philosophical-historical-international-studies/eras/past-editions/edition-six-2004-november/race-in-late-antique-egypt-moses-the-black-and-authentic-historical-voice [accessed 04 November 2022].

[84] *Vita di Mosè l'Etiope*, 55.

Chapter Three: Who Was Abba Moses

Whiteness was indeed a reflection of one's state of purity. The scribe who introduces this version of the biography is not so much concerned with the color of his skin to identify his race, rather that this natural feature of a person is employed metaphorically to portray a spiritual message. The symbolism using skin color is not meant to degrade him, on the contrary, it is used to sketch the excellence of his spiritual warfare. The Coptic *Doxology* 2.2 states that after he was baptized, "he became white like snow." In fact, it follows the biblical idea that white is a symbol of purity and spotlessness.[85] If I may suggest, it is similar to one saying: *Moses had a very dark past. Whereas now, he lives in the light!*

In two other occasions in the story of his ordination to the priesthood, one is faced with yet another encounter where the scribe of MS G makes Abba Moses himself play with this black/white symbolism. After ordaining him, the Pope dresses him in the liturgical vestment and says,

> "Behold, you are all white, O Moses." To which the elder responded, "I wonder, O Master and Patriarch, whether [this whiteness] is external or internal?"[86]

In a continuing incident, the patriarch wishes to test Abba Moses and alerts the priests not to allow him inside the sanctuary. If he

---

[85] Cf. Ps. 51:7, Is. 1:18, Rev. 3:5 and 6:11.

[86] *Vita di Mosè l'Etiope*, 95.

entered, he instructed them to tell him, "Get out of here, black man!" They did this and the scribe has managed to again use his skin color as a figurative image of his repentance. After Moses walked away, he thought,

> They treated you just as you deserved, O black one, covered in ashes and dirt. Indeed, you are not worthy of this great and honorable rank. (§20)

It was even said that Abba Moses used to tell his disciples, "My body and my soul are black."[87] In the melody that is composed to venerate him, the same imagery is seen once more when he confesses his sins to Abba Macarius, and Melody (14) states,

> Lo, an angel of light ✢ wiped away his black sins ✢
>
> The tablet became pure white ✢
>
> ⲡⲓϫⲱⲣⲓ ⲁⲃⲃⲁ ⲙⲱⲥⲏ (The Strong Abba Moses)

His worthiness is certainly not a result of his skin color, but because of his sublime humility to accept ridicule and self-examination. Therefore, the color white, being a symbol of purity, plays on the blackness of Moses' past life.[88]

---

[87] MS B–M. *Vita di Mosè l'Etiope*, 68.

[88] An analysis on the literary theory of the "blackness" of Moses can be read in Jean-Jacques Aubert, "La pertinence de la négritude: Moïse l'Ethiopien", in *Histoire et herméneutique. Mélanges offerts à G. Hammann*, vol. 3 (Labor et Fides, 2002): 27–40.

Chapter Three: Who Was Abba Moses

The next aspect that should be considered, and has been a topic of much debate, is his ethnicity. The two earliest sources—Palladius and Sozomen—both conflict on this matter. Palladius begins his entry by stating that Abba Moses is "Ethiopian by race." It was suggested that he is known as *the Ethiopian* because of his dark skin, and that he did not actually come from Ethiopia as we know it today, but that he originally belonged to one of the tribes along the Nile who pursued livestock, agriculture and robbery and whose citizens were usually tall and black.[89] Another suggestion comes from the hymnographical tradition that mentions he was a proto-thief in Gaza (*Doxology* 2.3). His race is not mentioned in the Coptic Synaxarium, only his skin color.[90] There is now widespread agreement among recent thought that Abba Moses was in fact from Nubia, and that the mention of "Ethiopian" only refers to his skin color.[91] Bishop Makarios, the bishop of the Diocese of Minya, endorsed this and wrote:

---

[89] Kathleen O'Brien Wicker, "Ethiopian Moses (Collected Sources)", *Ascetic Behavior in Greco-Roman Antiquity: A Sourcebook* (1990): 329–348.

[90] Rene Basset (ed.), *Le synaxaire arabe jacobite (rédaction copte) V. Les mois de Baounah, Abib, Mesoré et jours complémentaires*, PO 17 (Paris 1923) 591–594, edition in Arabic with a French translation, based on two manuscripts from the collection Paris, Bibliothèque Nationale, Fond arabe – no. 256 from the 16th century and no. 4780 from the end of the 14th century.

[91] See, Richter, Siegfried G., "The Beginnings of Christianity in Nubia," in Gawdat Gabra (ed.), *Christianity and Monasticism in Aswan and Nubia* (Cairo, 2013; online edn, Cairo Scholarship Online, 18 Sept. 2014),
https://doi.org/10.5743/cairo/9789774165610.003.0006, accessed 28 Oct. 2022.

> Moses was called *al-Aswad* because of the blackness of his skin, but he is not an Abyssinian [Ethiopian], and he is not a Berber either—as these were attacking Egypt from Libya. The word "Berber" was applied to the attackers of the country in general. It is likely that he is from Nubia, in the far south of Egypt, especially since he was a worshipper of the sun, whose devotion was common in ancient Egypt.[92]

This is also confirmed in another translation of *Moses 3*, where his virtue of silence is tested at an assembly of monks. The monks say to him, "Why does this Nubian person sit in our midst."[93]

In the *Sīra* of our book, the only indication we have about his origins is by the identification of his previous idolatry to the sun and fire with a specific mention of the *Maǧūsiyān Fārsiyyān* (Mazdean Zoroastrian) (§4), whereas in another part of the *Sīra*, he is said to have been enslaved by a man who was a *Ṣābī* (§7), a worshipper of planets. Both religions were well known in Egypt. Yet, it is difficult to deduce the exact origins of Abba Moses from these. He was most likely required to frequently move locations to avoid being captured for his crimes. Regardless, we know he ended up in Egypt and specifically *Wādī an-Naṭrūn*. From that moment onward, this became his dwelling place.

---

[92] Bishop Makarios, *al-Qawī al-Qidīs al-Anbā Mūsa al-Aswad* (Cario, 2006), 4.
[93] *Bustān*, 100 (179).

CHAPTER FOUR
SPIRITUAL STRUGGLE IN THE WILDERNESS

> Judas was in the company of Christ's disciples, and the Robber was in the company of murderers. And what a reversal when the crisis came!
>
> — John Climacus[94]

The persistent temptations that Abba Moses endured were indeed what shaped him into a fount of virtues. He himself stated, "If it were not for battles and struggles, there would not be virtue." (Isaiah 16.6)

Abba Moses was not the typical case of those who were called into the wilderness. We gather that his calling was a kind of *epiphany* which led him to pursue a life of repentance. There is no mention of any person persuading him, nor a monk's life which inspired him. His conversion was merely "by the command of God"

---

[94] John Climacus, *The Ladder of Divine Ascent*, Archimandrite Lazarus Moore (trans.), (Boston, Massachusetts: Holy Transfiguration Monastery, 2012), Step 10.4.

(Antiphonarium). In MS B–M, the epiphany comes in a single statement which reads:

> At last, God led him to repentance.[95]

The other account in MS G states:

> Thus, the evil he committed soon grew in the sight of God. So, God allowed him to become momentarily fatigued, restrained his mind and senses, and planted in him a righteous intention.[96]

The "righteous intention" is his calling into the wilderness. It appears earlier and more clearly in our *Sīra*:

> Our saint continued to behave in this way for a long time, but the One who knows the unknown, who does not wish death for the sinner, but that they return and live, looked upon this saint and awakened his conscience from its foolish state and a righteous intention came to him. (§5)

Our text continues with the idea that he simply *knew* what he was supposed to do. This kind of epiphany was known by the desert fathers and was even addressed by one of the elders in a Syriac apophthegm (see Chapter 6: "*An Elder 2*"). The elder states that there are three ways to which one is called to the monastic life. There is the "sudden calling" which is the case of Abba Moses, the "hearing

---

[95] *Vita di Mosè l'Etiope*, 57.
[96] *Vita di Mosè l'Etiope*, 83.

of Scripture" as in the case of Abba Antony and Abba Simeon the Stylite, and the "doctrine of the word" like the case of Abba Serapion and Abba Bessarion. In all three however, Divine Grace moves their conscience toward sincere and true repentance if they are willing to accept it.

When Abba Moses moved to *Wādī an-Naṭrūn,* he went to Abba Isidore the Priest (+390), who was the abbot of a community of monks at the time.[97] This elder portrays an important role in the life of Abba Moses as his spiritual guide. In Budge's *Lives of the Fathers, Martyrs, and Other Principal Saints*, he writes concerning Abba Isidore:

> He was priest of Scetis, and hermit in that vast desert. He excelled in an unparalleled gift of meekness, continency, prayer, and recollection. Once perceiving in himself some motions of anger to rise, he that instant threw down certain baskets he was carrying to the market and ran away to avoid the occasion. When in his old age, others persuaded him to abate something in his labor, he answered, "If we consider what the Son of God has done for us, we can never allow ourselves any indulgence in sloth. Were my body burnt, and my ashes scattered in the air, it would be nothing." Whenever the enemy tempted him to despair, he said, "Were I to be damned, you would yet be below me in hell; nor would I cease

---

[97] Abba Isidore appears in Cassian's Conferences adjoining the story of Abba Paphnutius, his successor in Conferences XV, *Of the example of patience given by Abbot Paphnutius*.

to labor in the service of God, though assured that this was to be my lot." If he was tempted to vain glory, he reproached and confounded himself with the thought, how far even in his exterior exercises he fell short of the servants of God, Antony, Pambo, and others. Being asked the reason of his abundant tears, he answered, "I weep for my sins. If we had only once offended God, we could never sufficiently bewail this misfortune." He died a little before the year 391.[98]

Abba Isidore was a companion to Abba Macarius, and no doubt learned from his spiritual knowledge and life in the desert. He instructs Abba Moses to stay in the wilderness and warns him that his previous life will most definitely haunt him. But Abba Isidore inspires hope in him and says, "If you remain the rest of your days here, I believe that God will have mercy on you" (§8). Being discipled by Abba Isidore, Abba Moses would receive instruction from a well-established desert father who triumphed over desire and temptation by determination and persistence; a factor that seems to have been inherited by Abba Moses.

We are then told that Abba Moses went to build his own cave where he could struggle against his desires (§9). In the *Apophthegmata Patrum*, Abba Moses receives this instruction from

---

[98] Alban Butler, *The Lives of the Fathers, Martyrs, and Other Principal Saints: Compiled from Original Monuments and Other Authentic Records, Illustrated with the Remarks of Judicious Modern Critics and Historians* (London: John Murphy, 1812), 193.

Chapter Four: Spiritual Struggle in the Wilderness

Abba Macarius who tells him to dwell in Petra, and there, he will find peace (Macarius the Egyptian 22).

It was important for the monk to dwell in a cell.[99] The purpose of the cell for the monk was threefold: 1) Devotion in prayer and conversation with God, 2) devoid of any distractions from the outside world, and 3) mortification of the body. These cells were small in both height and width.[100] Hermits lived in cells or caves encompassing two or more rooms, one of which functioned as an *oratory*.[101] Abba Moses himself, having experienced the effect of the cell, told a brother, "Go, and stay in a cell; your cell will teach you everything" (Moses 6).[102] Many of the Desert Fathers taught of the cell's significance. For example, the following is a list of his contemporaries speaking of the cell:

---

[99] Here I would like to recommend the chapter "Life in the Cell" from Lucien Regnault who offers an insightful entry on the practicalities of basketry: *The Day-to-Day Life of the Desert Fathers in Fourth-Century Egypt*, (Massachusetts: St. Bede's Publications), 82–95.

[100] Darlene L. Brooks Hedstrom has completed much research on the architecture of the cell and its relationship to monastics. See, "Your cell will teach you all things": The relationship between monastic practice and the architectural design of the cell in Coptic monasticism, 400–1000. (Ph.D. Diss, Miami University, Department of History, 2001).

[101] Gawdat Gabra, *Coptic Monasteries: Egypt's Monastic Art and Architecture* (Oxford University Press, 2002), 65.

[102] A suggested reading to understand how the cell affects the life of the monastic is Maria Giulia Genghini, "'Go, sit in your cell, and your cell will teach you everything' (AP Moses 6): How the Physical Environment Shaped the Spirituality of Early Egyptian Monasticism", *Studia Patristica. Vol. XCI: Papers Presented At the Seventeenth International Conference On Patristic Studies Held In Oxford 2015*, ed., Markus Vinzent (Leuven: Peeters, 2017).

1. "Flee from folk; remain in your cell; weep for your sins; take no delight in human conversation—and you are being saved." Abba Macarius the Egyptian[103]
2. "Go: eat, drink, sleep, do no work—only do not be out of your cell." Abba Arsenius[104]
3. "The person who learns the sweetness of the cell does not dishonor his neighbor in avoiding him." Abba Theodore of Phermē[105]
4. "There is a person who spends a hundred years in his cell and does not learn how one should live in a cell." Abba Ammonas[106]
5. "My son, if you want to receive benefit, persevere in your cell, paying attention to yourself and to your handiwork. [Coming out] does not procure you such benefit as staying inside." Abba Serapion[107]

The cell, to the secular world, is more than often portrayed as a place of detention; a room for those deemed guilty of the most heinous crimes; a home to murderers, thieves, and all sorts of unlawful offenders; even possibly as a space for the outcasts of

---

[103] *Give me a Word*: Macarius the Egyptian 41, 192.

[104] *Give me a Word:* Arsenius 11, 42.

[105] [pronounced Pherma]. *Give me a Word*: Theodore of Phermē 14, 120.

[106] *Give me a Word*: Poemen 95, 243.

[107] *Give me a Word*: Serapion 4, 298.

society. Indeed, Abba Moses was all of these, but was the cell really his place of detention?[108]

A life in the monastic cell was completely voluntary. It was the battleground for the monk to wage war against vice. There is the cell and there is the inner cell. For many, the inner cell is the secret place the Lord Jesus taught his disciples to pray. It is our own prayer room. It is that holy place where one can come to meet and talk to God. The cell is where the monk can examine himself, allowing God to search the heart and mind to struggle toward holiness and become holiness to the world. Abba Paul of Tamma states:

> You shall be a wise man in your cell, building up your soul as you sit in your cell, while glory is with you, while humility is with you, while the fear of God surrounds you day and night, while cares are thrown down, while your soul and your thoughts watch God in astonishment, gazing at him all the days of your life. [109]

Simply, it is the place where one comes to know God and be in communion with Him. The cell ... can be anywhere!

---

[108] I published an opinion article on VOX (University of Divinity) on Abba Paul of Tamma's extraordinary and deeply profound reflection on the cell. It is titled, "To the cell for you!": https://vox.divinity.edu.au/opinion/to-the-cell-for-you/

[109] Alin Suciu, "Sitting in the cell: the literary development of an ascetic praxis in Paul of Tamma's writings. With an edition of some hitherto unknown fragments of De cella," *The Journal of Theological Studies* 68, no. 1 (2017): 141-171.

In his cell, Abba Moses struggled greatly with *logismoi*, or *afkār* (thoughts) as translated into Arabic. It is any activity of the mind,[110] both good and bad. Bad *logismoi* is said to be the work of demons. There are *logismoi* of greed, laziness, unbelief, blasphemy, *porneia* and *accidie*.

The one temptation that is overly highlighted in the case of Abba Moses is the *logismoi* of *porneia*.[111] This is any and every elicit sexually or erotically associated activity in thought, word, or deed. An elder said:

> We experience these because of our negligence, for if we were convinced that God dwells within us, we would admit no alien matter to our person. [112]

The extent to which Abba Moses suffered this type of *logismoi* almost killed him (§11–15). He knew and taught that one's heart needs to be courageous when confronting *logismoi* (Isaiah 16.5). Of course, the voluntary life spent in the cell led a monk to be in the company of nothing else other than the *logismoi*. Spending time in

---

[110] Wortley leaves these words untranslated because of the wide meaning they bear. The definition he provides is: *logismoi* (pl.) a word of many meanings: it can simply mean one's thinking process, but it can also mean everything that goes on in that process, good, bad and indifferent, from a mere whim to a serious temptation. See, *An Introduction to the Desert Fathers*. (UK: Cambridge University Press, 2019), xvi. He has also provided an expounded definition in Chapter 4 "Impediments to Progress", 42–43.

[111] Wortley, "Chapter 4: Impediments to Progress", *An Introduction to the Desert Fathers* (UK: Cambridge University Press, 2019), 43–44.

[112] Wortley, "Chapter 4: Impediments to Progress", 45.

combat of anything entering the mind is essential to attaining virtue (Isaiah 7) and the discipline of the *logismoi* can only be done in silence with knowledge (Isaiah 16.7).

Abba Isidore had already warned Abba Moses that his previous life will most certainly haunt him, and haunt him it did! MS G states that Abba Isidore believed these were a result of a lingering imagination:

> This has caught up with you because you did not draw your mind away from imagination (*al-khayālāt*). For this is a hedge against you. But remove your thoughts from that which is fanciful (*al-fanṭassiya*), and you will rest by the grace of God. [113]

When he realized that he was losing the warfare against *porneia* he went to Abba Isidore who leaves him with a comforting word and asks him to return to his cell. His emotional exhaustion is expressed when he replied, "Abba, I cannot!" The extent to which he struggled against this sin led to the famous story found in *Moses 1* of the Apophthegmata.[114] The purpose is to emphasize that support in the spiritual struggle is an ever-present reality. If we are to believe the words of the Apostle Paul who said, "For we do not wrestle against flesh and blood, but against the rulers, against the authorities, against the cosmic powers over this present darkness, against the

---

[113] *Vita di Mosè l'Etiope*, 91.
[114] See also the version in the Arabic *Sīra* §27.

spiritual forces of evil in the heavenly places" (Eph. 6:12), then there should be confidence in the support from God's own ministers—spiritual, living, and departed. So, not only does one have the prayers and encouragement of their spiritual father, but also reassurance that the saints and spiritual beings support the repentant against every confronting evil. They are there even when one does not see them (Isaiah 16.9). Abba Isidore believed this and so did Abba Moses. His experience with the angels would eventually lead him to teach about the journey of the soul with the angels after death. He taught that the soul is accompanied by the angels into God's Kingdom, rejoicing for every good deed committed for the sake of Christ. Meanwhile, demons are finding any reason to accuse the soul and lead it to destruction (Isaiah 16.2).

The reference to angels appears two other times with Abba Moses. In *Arsenius 38*, Abba Arsenius is pictured in a vision with the Spirit of God while Abba Moses is with the angels of God.[115] The representation of the former is to highlight his spiritual wisdom and the latter underscores a soldier for Christ. The other reference appears in Coptic hymnography whereby Abba Moses confesses to Abba Macarius and an angel appears with a tablet to wipe away his sins.[116]

---

[115] *Arsenius 38*
[116] This can be found in both melodies in Chapter 8 of this book.

Chapter Four: Spiritual Struggle in the Wilderness

Though Abba Moses only discovered the spiritual support of the angels later in his struggle, he had already been aware of God's Divine support. When he first moved into his new cave, he was troubled by thirst and the lack of water. In MS B–M, we read that he prayed about this, and God answered saying,

> "O Moses, dwell there with joy and do not worry about the water." He immediately obeyed the voice and brought a pitcher full of water which he would drink from for several days. There always remained a small amount of water in it.[117]

At this point, we are first introduced to the ascetical practice which he observed to discipline his passions. Our *Sīra* tells us that he dug for himself a well forty cubits deep. During the evenings, he would go by the cells of the monks, take their jars, fill them up from his cistern and return the jars to the elders. MS G identifies this as his opportunity to perform an act of charity and service to the elderly monks:

> Since the elders needed water, and by virtue of the distance of the well, especially for hermits who were unable to carry water, he would minister to them this. Two kilometers away, and sometimes he travelled three kilometers carrying the jars, other times five

---

[117] *Vita di Mosè l'Etiope*, 58.

kilometers, sometimes six depending on the cell of each of the monks.[118]

This form of service was intended to distract him from Satan's temptations of *porneia*, especially since he performed these works at night or during the early morning. The notable aspect of this particular manual labor is that it was unrequested. Normally, the spiritual elder provides the work to be performed by the novice. Abba Moses was known to perform excessive works against the advice of his spiritual father—a matter that will be discussed later.

Perhaps it was charity that combatted his past practice of thievery? Certainly, this was part of the story; Moses the Robber is now Moses the Philanthropist. In MS G, the job of filling up water takes an ironic spotlight. The well-known story of his own robbery mentioned in §10 is said, in MS G, to have taken place while he was out filling up jars with water.[119] Even the story of his physical beating by Satan which left him completely unconscious and fractured happened while he was filling up water for the brethren (§11). Appropriate to mention here are his words: "He who endures injustice for the sake of the Lord is considered a martyr" (Isaiah 16.1). That Abba Moses was charitable meant that he was not quick

---

[118] *Vita di Mosè l'Etiope*, 86.
[119] *Vita di Mosè l'Etiope*, 86.

Chapter Four: Spiritual Struggle in the Wilderness

to judge (§10) and hospitable (§ 22 & 23). The late Sister Benedicta Ward (1993-2022) describes this concept:

> The aim of the monks' lives was not asceticism, but God, and the way to God was charity. The gentle charity of the desert was the pivot of all their work and the test of their way of life. Charity was to be total and complete.[120]

A closer look at the manual labor which Abba Moses performed indicates that they were indeed acts of charity; deeds committed in secret (Cf. Matt. 6:1-4). He taught this when he said:

> Give to the needy with pleasure and contentment, lest you be ashamed among the saints and deprived of their glories. (Isaiah 16.4)

> It is better for you to work with your hands so that the poor may take bread from you… (Isaiah 16.9)

His other form of manual labor was weaving baskets. This was perhaps one of the most common forms of manual labor in monastic life.[121] Weaving baskets was an important and profitable work since people needed them to transport basic commodities. It was a convenient labor that could be used by monks to busy their time so that they did not fall into *accidie*, and it also provided them with an

---

[120] Benedicta Ward, *The Sayings of the Desert Fathers*, xxiv.

[121] Regnault offers an insightful entry on the practicalities of basketry: *The Day-to-Day Life of the Desert Fathers in Fourth-Century Egypt*, 99 - 102.

income to support the brethren. This task was always accompanied by meditation and was never to be completed without prayer, otherwise the mind would become an open field for Satan. A story about Abba John Colobos tells us that he "was weaving rope for two baskets, but he made it into one without noticing, until it had reached the wall, because his *logismoi* was occupied in contemplation." [122] Contemplation was the intention of manual labor, and Abba Moses taught this as well:

> Charity with knowledge gives birth to contemplation of what is to come and leads one to glory. (Isaiah 16.6)

Abba Moses learned to weave baskets in response to a vicious attack from Satan that left him completely battered. His determination led him to complete thirty baskets a day. The account in MS G states that his *logismoi* overpowered him, planting a seed of doubt: "How long will this labor last that you should die before your time comes?"[123] Those words afflicted him and caused him to decrease in his manual labor until "his soul was melting with the desire to fornicate,"[124] plunging all hope. Immediately, he sought the direction of his spiritual father who comforted and counselled him. "The demons," Abba Isidore said, "wage war on you because you are

---

[122] *Give me a Word*, John Colobos 11, 133.
[123] *Vita di Mosè l'Etiope*, 88–89.
[124] *Vita di Mosè l'Etiope*, 89.

a novice at the beginning of your training."[125] To educate him, Abba Isidore explained that Satan is like a dog who waits outside the slaughterhouse, waiting for the butcher to throw out the meat. But the butcher does not entertain the dog's desire and does not open the door for the dog to enter and feast on the meat. When the dog realizes that the butcher is not relenting, he leaves. After receiving this counsel, Abba Moses returned to his cell feeling strengthened. However, *logismoi* from his previous life continued to taunt him through his dreams. It seemed, to Abba Moses, that there was no way of ridding himself of these and he was falling into great despair.

The scribe of MS G, using Abba Moses, wishes to paint his spiritual passion as a relatable struggle to readers and listeners of his biography. It is not normal that a person overcomes the passions of their past overnight; persistence and determination are crucial for the attainment of virtue.

After receiving a comforting word from Abba Isidore, he returned to his cell and resumed his ascetical practice to the extent that "his body was extremely weakened" (§14). Abba Isidore comforts him a second time, and he continues this for six years, keeping vigil and going for long walks at night so as not to fall into any kind of temptation. Abba Isidore notices his struggle, as MS G states:

---

[125] *Vita di Mosè l'Etiope*, 89–90.

Abba Isidore said to him, "O Moses, stop fighting the devils, humanity have a limit to their devotion. Unless God has mercy on you and keeps them away from you, then it is impossible to fight them because they are spirits, and you are only a physical human being. Go, and humbly hand your request to God. When God sees your patience, He will have mercy on you. For it is impossible that a person lives without dreams, but the power of the mind is for a person to escape from the imagination. One should not worry if he comes across fantastical thoughts and should consider them to be like a passing wind. If they visit you, and you do not accept them, they will disappear."

Abba Moses said to him, "I will never abandon my determination to worship God until this war is released from me." So, the elder replied, "Listen to me, O Moses: Go to your cell and seek help in these matters in humility before God. And from now on, I believe in my Lord Jesus Christ, that He will quickly nullify these dreams from you, they will no longer fight you, and a righteous revelation will come upon you. Come, take your needs from the Holy Mysteries, for these dreams are overpowering you. You say, 'my thoughts are unclean, so how can I partake from the Holy Mysteries when I am not clean?' What the demons want is for our hearts to become defiled so that we do not raise our faces and partake of the Holy Mysteries. If we ignore their appeals, they will go away on their own." And so, he took Abba Moses into the

> church, and they approached [the Eucharist]. After this, Abba
> Moses went to his cave, thanking God, and rested.[126]

A Syriac *apophthegm* wanted to teach the brethren this same message, using the example of Abba Moses, that manual labor is not enough to overcome *logismoi*; one requires the active work of the Spirit (see Chapter 6: "*An Elder 1*"). This explains why Abba Isidore formerly asked him to lessen his ascetic practices. Abba Moses, bearing a physically healthy body, had immensely focused on the exhaustion of the body through manual labor to overcome sin. He forgot that the Spirit of God is He who inspires change in a person, and not one's ascetical labor alone. Indeed, he learned that one who does not perform manual labor causes death to the soul (Isaiah 16.2), hence it is necessary for salvation (Isaiah 7).

One should note the special placement of the Eucharist in this story, and it seems that this was done intentionally. That Abba Moses was instructed to partake of the communion after a long warfare with evil passions, is of itself a lesson to the readers. The scribe adds a unique question about an individual's spiritual condition before approaching the Eucharist which does not exist in any other version of the biography. Indeed, the question of worthiness is still asked today. But the scribe wants his readers to know that abstinence, which is not a recommendation of the

---

[126] *Vita di Mosè l'Etiope*, 92–93.

spiritual father, serves the purpose of the demons who enjoy polluting the heart. The scribe's approach to tackle the question of unworthiness does not focus on how a person is made worthy, instead it affirms the quest for a monk to defeat the wiles of Satan. The expression "raising our faces" refers to the believer's approach to the Eucharist in complete confidence that Christ is the conqueror of Satan and puts to naught our sins. The conclusion of several fraction prayers in the Divine Liturgy affirms this and states:

> …that with a pure heart, an enlightened conscience, **an unashamed face,** a faith unfeigned, a perfect love, and a firm hope…

In the story, the message is clear: only after a devout and sincere repentance, a real struggle against sin, does the Eucharist become the medicine that would overcome one's battles and extends rest to the heart. After partaking of the Eucharist, we no longer hear that Abba Moses struggled with sin, rather when Abba Isidore enquires about his condition, he responds:

> "I thank God for your prayers, my saintly father. From now on, I am no longer scared of demons. They are now to me like passing flies." (§16)

This story further points to a remarkable lesson on the partaking of the Holy Mysteries. The Eucharist should be approached by those who are truly repentant and have struggled against a particular sin.

It is true repentance that allows for the movement of the Spirit to change and refocus the condition of one's heart. Abba Moses does not learn how to combat Satan on his own, rather this work is revealed to him through the partaking of the Eucharist. From the moment Abba Moses partakes of the Eucharist, the biographer no longer speaks about his struggle, and instead places the attention to his glory. A similar pattern is seen in the *Life of Abba Antony*, who describes his first temptation in this way:

> ...this was Antony's first struggle against the devil, or rather this victory was the Savior's work in Antony ...[127]

This telling statement by St Athanasius (†373) intends to juxtapose the initial perception of the spiritual struggle to the truth behind ascetical battles: the work of Christ within us. When Abba Isidore tells Abba Moses, "I believe that God will have mercy on you," we are witnessing a foreshadow of his victory over sin, acknowledging that his struggle is indeed the furnace of the Savior's work in molding the golden heart of Abba Moses.

Foundations of the Spiritual Life

After his ordination to the priesthood (§20), the scribes of the *Sīra* begin to focus on his miracles and teachings. But his ordination was not due to his overcoming of sin, rather, his words and deeds

---

[127] Vivian and Athanassakis (trans.,), *The Life of Antony: The Coptic Life and Greek Life*, 72.

inspired so many around him, seeing him become a spiritual leader, elder, and teacher to a community of monks. MS B–M describes how the monks would sit around him while he taught them and guided them in matters pertaining to the salvation of their soul:

> He advised them to lend their ears to the divine words and to act in accordance with them; to achieve obedience and humility by which the power of demons is driven out; to cover the sins of our brothers and not announce them,[128] so that God may cover our sins. [He taught them to] love our brothers and never expose them so that God protects the good Christians who worship Him. He taught them not to despise the misguided but to teach them with love and plead that God may guide them to the true faith.[129]

The spiritual teachings of Abba Moses were most certainly influenced by his own struggle, experience, and divine revelation. His principles for the monks were centered around unity in Christ through practical methods that defeat the body's desire to pursue the heart's zeal toward God. As mentioned earlier, three elements are highlighted in his discourses: 1) the fear of God, 2) deep contemplation of God, and 3) knowledge of God. They are not separate in principle, but a means to the same goal—God.

---

[128] A lesson that was also taught by Abba Macarius. Cf. *Give me a Word,* Macarius the Egyptian 32, 188.

[129] *Vita di Mosè l'Etiope,* 67.

The fear of God (*al-khawf min Allah*) is tantamount for one to be encouraged in the spiritual journey. Abba Moses understood the fear of God to be the only way a person considers Satan's evil works as a speck before God's grace (cf. Isaiah 16.2). "This is because the fear of God is preservation and care for the mind," (Isaiah 16.5) he says, and a lack of the fear of God prevents one's mind from acquiring knowledge and meditation on God. Knowledge (Arabic: *ma'rifa*, Coptic: ⲅⲛⲱⲥⲓⲥ) was a well-known concept among monastic and patristic circles.[130] Acquiring knowledge is both a condition and practice. Through the example of Mary and Martha, Abba Moses taught that though Martha was performing an act of sacred service to Christ, Mary was intent on spiritual instruction "clinging to the feet of Jesus which she kissed and anointed with the ointment of a good confession."[131] Mary, he says, performs "divine meditation" or "contemplation," a condition that will last forever. His treatment of this begins with practical methods that allow for the novice to take small steps by first "reflecting on a few saints" that will eventually lead the monk to the sole contemplation of God alone; "so as to get beyond those actions and services of saints, and feed on the beauty and knowledge of God alone." Believing that a monk should continually cling to Christ, he also understands its difficulty because

---

[130] Fr. Mark Sheridan commented on the usage of this work in the works of 6th-century bishop, Rufus of Shotep. See, *Rufus of Shotep: Homilies on the Gospels of Matthew and Luke; introduction, text, translation, commentary* (Roma: CIM, 1998), 251–252.

[131] *Conference I*, chapter 8.

of the human flesh that weighs down every person. But that does not mean that one should not struggle toward this state. He considers the need for one to be reminded of the soul's continual gaze on Christ, fixing the heart only on Him, "considering that even a momentary departure from gazing on Christ is fornication."[132] And since "the Kingdom of God is within you" (Luke 17:21), the quest is to prepare the soul through knowledge and virtue for the indwelling of God's Kingdom, as opposed to "ignorance of truth and vice" for Satan's kingdom. Knowledge and deep contemplation are allies to bringing one into the fullness of God. Abba Moses sees three practical ways one may meditate on God: Discovering God through contemplating His incomprehensible essence, "a matter hidden in the hope of the promise,"[133] which is the indwelling of God in us as His chosen vessel;[134] admiring His creation and marveling at the greatness of God's work in nature;[135] and pondering the justice of God in the saints and His daily providence in our lives that leads one to imitate their lives and experience God's ineffable mercy in our repentance of sin. Abba Moses learned that defeating bad *logismoi* (thoughts) was to fill one's mind with *gnosis* (knowledge) in their place. The simple and practical remedy to perfect these three is the

---

[132] *Conference* I, chapter 13.
[133] *Conference* I, chapter 15.
[134] See *Conference* I, chapter 19.
[135] Abba Moses himself did this in his soliloquy (§5 & §6).

mere reading of scripture, psalm singing, fasts, and vigils,[136] the very prescription of the Church today.

Martyr for Christ

The final moment of his life paints a courageous repentant, standing before the men who resembled the man he once was. It was the year AD 407 where a group of infamous Berbers known as Mazices[137] came attacking from the Libyan Desert, and confronted Abba Moses and seven disciples, murdering them all.[138] In the Coptic Synaxarium, an account describes a number of elders who visit Abba Macarius, who foretells, "I see among you one to whom belongs the crown of martyrdom."[139] But on the day of his martyrdom, Abba Moses knew that the Berbers' raid will be the moment of his divine judgement, quoting Matt. 26:52. He accepted martyrdom rather than raging war. Though one might count his unwillingness to fight against the Berbers as cowardice, it was his discipline that invited the Spirit to cultivate inner courage and peace to face this threat. His prior teachings are also an indication to his readiness to face the Berbers when he said, "Remembrance of judgment births the

---

[136] *Conference I*, chapter 17.

[137] Or Mastiki. The Coptic has ⲛⲓⲙⲁⲕⲓ. See White, *The Monasteries of Wadi 'N Natrûn. Part 1*, 140 n.2, 292; Y. Moderan, "Mazices, Mazaces", *Encyclopédie berbère* 31 (2010): 4799-4810.

[138] Palladius does not seem to be aware of the manner by which Abba Moses departed, only recording that he died at the age of 75 and left 70 monks behind.

[139] There is a Coptic oral tradition that identifies these elders as Abba Evagruis, Abba Cronius, Abba Pambo and three other Desert Fathers.

strength of God in the *logismoi*" (Isaiah 16.7). The portrayal we have is of one who had already known by divine providence the manner of his death. God prepared Abba Moses for this very moment.

He had previously warned the monks in a prophecy that the monastery would be devasted if the monks had not kept the ascetical practices and teachings of their fathers (Moses 6). The coming of the Berbers led many to flee, abandon Scetis, and pursue monasticism in Palestine and Gaza.[140] Now that Abba Moses is the proto-martyr of *Wādī an-Naṭrūn*, monks raised questions concerning the Berber invasions and physical martyrdom. Abba Sisoes (†429), who himself witnessed several devastations of monastic settlements by the Berbers was asked:

> "I am residing in the desert and a barbarian comes by wanting to kill me, shall I kill him if I am able?" "No," said the elder, "hand him over to God. For whatever temptation comes upon a person, let him say, 'It is on account of my sins that this has happened.' But if it is a good thing, 'This is by the providence of God!'"[141]

Abba Moses became the image of what it means to struggle against sin, even to the point that he was first spiritually martyred, then physically martyred. At the climax of his biography, a contrast of one person unfolds, fulfilling the words of the Gospel and the

---

[140] The Apophthegmata gives the example in Anoub 1 and Daniel 1.

[141] *Give me a Word*, Sisoes 34, 289.

prophecy by Abba Moses that "he who lives by the sword, dies by the sword" (Matt. 26:52). At first, we are introduced to a vengeful and wrathful Moses, carrying a sword in his mouth as he crosses the river to slaughter the shepherd. By the end, we are faced with the humble and meek Abba Moses, who carries nothing but the word of Christ in his mouth.

I will now leave the reader to meditate on the life and sayings of Abba Moses and learn from his spiritual wisdom.

Figure 1.

13th c. wall painting of Abba Moses the Black at St Antony's Monastery in the Red Sea, Egypt. Photo by the author.

CHAPTER FIVE
THE LIFE OF ABBA MOSES

In the name of the Holy Divinity, One God,
Creator of Creation.

§1. The *Life* comprising the struggle of the courageous Abba Moses the Black who completed his righteous toil and received the crown of martyrdom on the 24th of the month of *Ba'ūna*.

§2. May his prayers be with us. Amen.

∴ **PROLOGUE**

§3. We must now inform you in a simple manner, O beloved brethren, about the struggle of our righteous and saintly father, the honored and elect vessel, Abba Moses the Black. Indeed, the [Holy] Book forbids us from speaking about thieves and fornicators, but we have instead decided to speak about their righteous return, to envy their repentance and desire their ways, as by the example of this honored saint.

§4. This Abba Moses was a slave to a man who was a colonel and who worshiped the fire and sun of the Mazdean Zoroastrian religion. His master was distressed because of his wickedness and the abundance of his evil deeds, and so expelled him. Thus, Moses went on to become the chief of thieves, for he was a courageous fighter and a great and skillful champion.

∴ MOSES AND THE SHEPHERD

It happened that one day he passed by a shepherd who was steering a flock of sheep. When the shepherd had seen the saint, he became fearful because of his dreadful appearance and released his dogs against Moses. This threat lingered in his mind every day and he sought to kill that shepherd. At a later time, someone had informed Moses about the hours in which the shepherd normally crosses the river. He quickly got up and went to cross the river. It was the time of the Nile and the river was significantly elevated, but Moses, tying a cloth around his head, and gripping a sword in his hand, crossed the river until he reached the shepherd.

When the shepherd spotted him, he quickly fled and left behind his sheep due to the severity of his fear. But Abba Moses the Black entered the sheep's barn, seized four large rams, the best of the flock of sheep, and slaughtered them. He tied them over a hook with a rope, then tied the rope around his waist and crossed the mighty sea, dragging the rams with him. His clothes were wrapped around his head and his sword was in his mouth.

When he reached land, Moses entered his cave, skinned the rams and ate a container worth of the best and most delicious parts of their flesh. He then collected the rest of the meat and sold it to buy wine with the profits. He drank twenty Egyptian portions of wine. He then took the skin of the rams, sold them, bought a container of wine that had three hundred and thirty portions. He carried it for seven days until he reached his robber companions and told them of all that had happened to him. They binged the rest of the wine together and were all overjoyed.

§5. This saint continued to behave in this way for a long time, but the One who knows the unknown, who does not wish death for the sinner but that they return and live, looked upon this saint and awakened his conscience from its foolish state, and a righteous intention came to him. He knew what he needed to do and hurriedly ventured into the wilderness of Scetis and to the cell of Abba Isidore the priest.

∴ THE SOLILOQUY

Moses stood outside the cell [of Abba Isidore] and cried out, "O God, who is unknown to me! Straighten my way to the path of salvation and peace, for I have come to You, O God of the monks. O Savior of the world, who saved the thief crucified on Your right and gave him the inheritance of the Kingdom of Heaven, guide me to the path that leads me into life and [teach me] the deeds that pleases You."

§6. When Abba Isidore came to leave his cell and go to the church, he came face to face with Abba Moses the Black and was frightened, because his appearance was strange and too terrifying. The priest Isidore asked, "What do you want from this place, my brother?" Moses replied, "I have heard that you are a righteous servant of God. For this reason, I have fled and come to you so that the God who saved you, may also save me. I beg, ask and prostrate before you, make me a monk. I have committed many sins and great evils!" But Abba Isidore responded, "Who brought you to this place?" Abba

Moses replied, "I heard about your reverence from a farmer whom I had met harvesting in a field. He told me, 'Go to Abba Isidore, and he will save your soul.' So here I am begging for the salvation of my soul. Do not reject me so that God does not ask you about my blood."

§7. Upon hearing these words Abba Isidore asked him, "What had you worshipped in this world?" Moses replied, "I had not known God. On the contrary, while I was sitting in the field, I turned my gaze to the sun and saw it illuminating the world with its radiance, but it disappeared in the evening causing darkness to everything it covered. So also was it with the moon and stars, there seemed a wondering mystery about them. Rain would fall heavily in the winter and very little in the summer. The temperature and radiance of the sun would intensify at times and diminish at another. I noticed all these things. Even the sea had a time where it would rise and other times where it would be in drought. I knew, then, that these matters must have a ruler, one who governs, who is a supreme being in the heavens. Thus, I left everything and thought to myself, 'O Lord, God, who dwells in heaven, He who guides all creation, guide me also to what pleases You.'

"Behold, I have now come before you, asking your reverence to come to my aid and beg God not to be angry with me because of my evil deeds nor to destroy me. For I have committed too many sins and every kind of wickedness." He said this with many tears.

The elder said, "What had you believed in, my son?" Abba Moses replied, "When I was in my region, I worshipped the fire. When they sold me in these lands, I became a slave to a master who was a [worshipper of] Ṣābī,[142] but I did not worship anything then."

§8. When Abba Isidore heard these words, he took him and entered the Church, baptizing him in the name of the Holy Trinity: The Father, the Son and the Holy Spirit. He clothed him with a robe and with the holy habit (the ʾiskīm) and taught him many lessons from the Holy Book. He commanded Abba Moses, saying, "Stay here, my son, in the wilderness. For the day on which you leave this wilderness all the evils that have haunted you will return to you once again. But if you remain the rest of your days here, I believe that God

---

[142] One who worships planets.

will be gracious and have mercy on you." Abba Moses accepted the words of Abba Isidore and lived with the brethren.

∴ THE SOLITUDE OF ABBA MOSES

§9. The enemy of good, who is Satan, did not tolerate the work of the holy Abba Moses and wrestled him with the ardent desire of fornication by reminding him of his previous conduct, making it seem pleasant to return to those pernicious things. But Abba Moses got up and quickly withdrew into the inner wilderness and dwelled in a cave that he built for himself. He dug a well into the ground that was forty cubits deep. He would often go in the night to the cells of the elder-monks, and take their empty jars, fill them with water, and place them at their doors. They would wake up in the morning to find the jars full and realize that it was Abba Moses who had done this, so they prayed for him and blessed him.

This saint would perform many acts of devotion. He endured four years without ever sleeping or sitting, but stood with both hands raised in prayer, begging God to remove the eager desire of fornication from him. He was so persistent that the diabolical temptations were eventually relieved.

∴ MOSES IS ROBBED

§10. One night, Abba Moses had left for the church. Our saint surprised some thieves who had entered his cell and stole everything that was there. As they were about to leave, he burst inside, tied the four robbers with a rope as if they were a log of wood, loaded them on his shoulders and carried them[143] down to the church, and set them before the elder saints, saying, "Bless me. I do not wish to accuse anyone. When I entered my cell, I found these people who robbed all that was in my cave. I limited myself to binding them like this, and did not discipline them, but brought them here in your presence. Do as you wish with them."

The thieves wondered who this man was, saying, "Tell us, who was that monk?" "This is Moses the Black. He used to be the chief of thieves," they replied. When the thieves heard these words, they prostrated before the monastic fathers and repented of their sins. They were then tonsured as monks at the place of Abba Moses and became ascetics and anchorites, walking in the commandments of the Lord.

---

[143] MS G: "carried them like little boys."

∴ ABBA MOSES AND *LOGISMOI*

§11. When Abba Moses had completed six years in devotion, the devil, although not tolerating his good works, had left him in peace, until one day, having gone to the well to draw some water, he brutally beat him with violent blows in his side until his bones were fractured. The holy Abba Moses fell to the ground like a dead man and could not move. In the morning the brethren came to the well to draw some water and found Abba Moses on the ground, laying there like a dead man. They went to the church of Abba Isidore the priest, and informed him saying, "Our father, that strange black man whom you tonsured a monk is now lying on the ground as a dead man by the well!"

Abba Isidore sent the brethren to carry him and bring him to the church. When they had done this, the elder saw him, and immediately knew that Satan had struck him because Abba Moses had not surrendered to Satan's perverse will.

The holy Abba Moses remained in that state for three days, until he awoke, although he was still frail and not yet able to stand up. Abba Isidore said to him, "Enough, O Moses, stop fighting Satan, lest he persecute you! Consider a path that is simpler like the rest of the brethren." "Was it Satan who struck me?" Abba Moses said. The elder replied, "Yes, it was the devil who did this, my son."

§12. Abba Moses became infuriated with Satan. He returned to his cave and learned to weave baskets. He weaved thirty baskets each day and ate an ounce of bread every day. When he approached a thousand baskets, he abandoned it because of the weakness of his heart. *Thoughts* began to overpower and discourage him, and he began weaving only ten baskets of palm leaves every day and ate five ounces of bread. It was to the extent that the thoughts of fornication became more and more obsessive, and evil spirits troubled him with many temptations.

§13. Not being able to handle it anymore and now eager to give in, he immediately got up and went to his father, Isidore the priest, and told him about all his thoughts. Abba Isidore said to him, "Do not let your heart be anxious about this warfare, my beloved son, and do not belittle yourself. This is what the devil normally commits with the elect of God. But as for you, persevere, do not be of two hearts, and the Lord will strengthen you. You have not followed the advice of those before you to defeat the enemy. I will tell you that Satan is like the dogs that wander around a slaughterhouse. The devils will kill you so that you return to your old habits. From now on be strong and do not let your heart be weakened. Know that God is able to take them away from you."

After he heard the words of Abba Isidore, he became extremely comforted and confident that God—by the prayers of his father, Abba Isidore—will put an end to Satan's guiles. So Abba Moses returned to his cell.

§14. Many were the devotional practices to which he dedicated himself. He no longer ate every day, except for an ounce of dry bread. He prayed fifty times day and night and accomplished three hundred prostrations. When his body became extremely weakened and the fierceness of thoughts and deceitful dreams increased, he went again to meet Abba Isidore the priest who blessed, comforted, and strengthened him and sent him back to his cell.

§15. He stayed for six years without ever sleeping and would stand all night in vigil. If sleep began to overpower him, he would walk from place to place. Abba Isidore once told him, "Moses, my son, stop fighting the devils! Even humans have a limit when it comes to devotion. Unless God has mercy on you and keeps them away from you, you will not be able to fight them. Go now, humble yourself and meeken your spirit, and hand your request to God. If God sees your patience, He will have mercy on you."

Abba Moses said to him, "My father, I will never abandon my warfare until it is released from me." "Go, my son. I believe in my Lord Jesus Christ, that He will quickly nullify these thoughts. Enter now into the holy church and partake of the Holy Mysteries, in order that it might cast the devils away from you," the elder responded.

§16. Thus, our saint did this and went to his cave, thanking God the Lord Christ. When Abba Moses had stayed for two months while committed to the words of the elder, God granted him great grace, humility, and internal calmness.

It happened that Abba Isidore visited him and asked, "How are you doing, O Abba Moses?" He replied, "I thank God for your prayers, my saintly father. From here on, I am no longer scared of the demons. They are now to me like passing flies." Abba Isidore responded, "Always be humble and meek in heart, and Christ the Lord will come to your aid." Dictating these things to him, he blessed Abba Moses and retired to his cell.

∴ THOSE WHO VISITED ABBA MOSES

§17. After some time, many people came to the mountain from Egypt bringing with them a number of weak people possessed with demons and all kinds of illnesses. One of them shouted, "O Abba Moses, have mercy on me and save me from the worship of Satan!" When the brothers heard these words, they knew that the Holy Spirit dwelt in Abba Moses.

∴ HEALING A COW

§18. One day, while the holy Abba Moses was walking in the wilderness, he saw a cow that had given birth to a calf but was unable to feed even a drop of milk. The holy Abba Moses gazed at the cow and felt empathy. Taking some water, he poured it over the cow and her baby, and the calf immediately went to his mother and began to drink her milk.

∴ HEALINGS

§19. Abba Moses would pass by those who were possessed by demons, pray over them and heal them, as if they had never experienced any suffering, and they went home perfectly healthy.

∴ ABBA MOSES ORDAINED A PRIEST

§20. One time, Abba Isidore took Abba Moses and ventured into the city of Alexandria. Abba Moses thought that it was for a spiritual reason until they arrived at the place of the patriarch who wanted to ordain him a priest. When they went with him before the altar, the patriarch[144] wanted to test him, and so said to the priests, "Get this black man out of here!" They did this and stood afar to observe how he would respond. They overheard his self-accusation, "They treated you just as you deserved, O black one, covered in dirt and ash. Indeed, you are not worthy of this great and honorable rank."

---

[144] Probably Theophilus. Archbishop from 384 to 412.

The patriarch then ordered to bring him back to his presence, laid his hand on him and ordained him a priest. Meanwhile, a voice came from on high saying: Worthy! Worthy! Worthy!

Our father the patriarch invoked him, saying, "O Moses, I tell you that as of this moment, you are now all white because you have received this distinguished rank of the priesthood. Therefore, carry out your ministry well, as is appropriate."

∴ MONASTERY OF *AL-BARAMŪS*

§21. After these things, he returned to the wilderness and his name became known in all regions of the world. He became a reputed [elder] among those who lived in the wilderness. Five hundred brethren became children of Abba Moses under his care. Today, the monastery bears his name *"al-Baramūs."*

∴ ABBA MOSES PRAYS FOR WATER

§22. One day, some brothers came to greet him. He set the table before them but found no water for them to drink. He began to walk in and out of his cell, and immediately God made rain fall from the sky so that the well was filled, and they drank. Then one of the brothers asked him, "Why did you walk in and out, father?" He replied, "I was talking with God, saying, 'If You do not give me water for Your servants to drink, where will I get water to offer them?'" And they were amazed at the purity of his heart.

∴ CONFRONTING CRAVINGS

§23. On another occasion, the brothers went to Abba Moses, and he set the table before them, placing a piece of roasted snake on it. The brothers wanted to eat, but the saint prevented them, saying, "Don't touch it, my brothers, it's an evil beast!" And the brothers asked him, "Why would you ever do such a thing, O our father?" And he replied to them, "Brothers, my poor soul was craving fish. I did this to subdue my desirous craving."

The brothers were greatly amazed and glorified God who bestowed on His saint this exceptional grace and the ability to withstand the trials of this life. He then delivered many homilies to them from Holy Scriptures on love and humility, teaching them that these are the pinnacle of good deeds and what will lead them into the grace of the Heavenly Kingdom.

∴ I AM WITH YOU

§24. Later, he decided to go into the inner desert to devote himself to God, when suddenly Satan came to him and said, "There is no water over there!" But a voice came from heaven that said, "Be strong, O My servant Moses. I will be with you unto the age of ages."

∴ THE DISOBEDIENT MONK

§25. One of the brothers who had fallen ill decided to go down into the Delta. Being aware of this situation, Abba Moses therefore came to him and said, "I beg you! Do not leave the monastery tonight so that you do not fall into the sin of fornication." To which that brother said to him, "Why would you pain my heart with your words, O pure father?" Our holy father left him and went his way.

§26. The monk then went down into the Delta where people went to see him and serve him. A young virgin also came to take his blessing, but he fell into sin with her, taking away her virginity, and he continued to sin with her for many days. Her father and family when they had a feeling as to what was happening, asked her, "Who has degraded you to such a state?" "It was the monk *so-and-so* who did this to me," she replied. Her parents confronted him, and he confirmed, "Yes, it was I who did such a thing."

After a short amount of time, she became pregnant and gave birth to a beautiful baby. They carried him to the [sinful] elder and he, taking the baby into his arms, went up to the desert and to the church where he laid the baby in front of the elders saying, "Look, O saintly fathers, this is a child of perversion and transgression, and this is the embarrassment that has fallen on me in my elderly age. Judge me, now, according to what I deserve." They then prescribed canons to him, and he retired into the wilderness to weep over his sin.

∴ GOD'S CHILDREN ARE SUPPORTED BY THE SAINTS

§27. One day, Abba Moses went to Abba Isidore and said, "My father, thoughts are deeply killing me." Taking him by the hand, he went up to the roof of the church and said to him, "Look west, my son." And behold, he saw Satan surrounded by his legions with a very black and hideous appearance. Then he looked east and saw a multitude of shining, white-robed angels glorifying the Holy Trinity. Abba Moses thanked God very much, and Abba Isidore said to him, "My son, those who are in the west are those who make war against the saints, while those in the east are those sent by God to help His elect."

∴ MOSES IS VISITED BY AN ARCHON

§28. One time, an archon from Cairo had heard of Abba Moses and ardently wanted to see him and receive his blessing, and so ventured into the desert. When Abba Moses heard of this, he fled from the archon into the valley. The archon happened to meet him on the way and, not knowing who he was, said, "O monk, where is Abba Moses and where is his cave?" The saintly Abba Moses responded, "What do you want from him? He is a poor and crazy person, a forsaken man[145] in this wilderness. He has no dwelling place to rest, and he roams around weeping over his sin."

After the saint had said these things, the archon went to the church, sat down and said to the brethren, "My saintly fathers, I came all the way here intending to take the blessing of the father, Abba Moses, and instead I found an elderly and saintly man on the road, wearing shabby and filthy clothing who said to me that the man I was looking

---

[145] Ar. *sāyib*

for is crazy and has no dwelling place." The brethren informed the archon that the man who told him these things was Abba Moses.

∴ MARTYRDOM AND EPILOGUE

§29. Later, the brothers gathered around him and sat on the floor to hear him speak of God from his pure mouth. He then said to them, "Brothers, the berbers have come. Whoever among you wishes to stay, then stay, but whoever wishes to flee, flee now." But some of them replied, "Why do you not flee, our father?" And he answered them saying, "My beloved children, this is the day I have been waiting for, because it is written, 'Whoever kills with the sword will be killed by the sword.'"[146]

The brothers fled and there were only seven left. The berbers broke into the monastery and found Abba Moses with those brothers and slaughtered them with swords on the rock of Amūn.

§30. They completed their struggle, obtaining the immortal crown in the Kingdom of Heaven on the 24th of the month of *Ba'ūna*. The Lord gave this Saint three crowns: the first, for his labors and his

---

[146] Matt. 26:52

ascetic practices; the second, for his monasticism and priesthood; the third, for having shed his pure blood.

§31. Now, O beloved brothers, look at the power of [his] repentance and what it has done: it has moved a slave, an infidel, murderer, thug, thief, profligate, fornicator, glutton, drunkard, pagan worshipper of the sun and of the created elements, and turned him into a monk, a teacher, a guide, a preacher of the gospel, an elect priest and a father of numerous souls whom he has saved by his prayers that God accepted. His name is celebrated on altars in every part of the earth.

∴ DOXOLOGY ON REPENTANCE

§32. O repentance, door of life!

O repentance, key to the Kingdom of heaven!

O repentance, which saves the soul from the judgment of hell!

O repentance, spiritual door that rises into heights!

O repentance, for through you fornicators are saved!

O repentance, for through you the evildoers are purified!

O repentance, for through you those who are defiled by sin have become pure!

O repentance, who raises to heaven and leads to paradise!

O repentance, for through you thieves have become righteous and sinners holy!

O repentance, who has turned the infidels into priests and teachers!

O repentance, who does not disappoint those who seek you and with which there is no judgment or punishment!

33. Let us draw near to repentance, therefore, and hasten to complete it with works even before words. Let us repent of our sins and advance to meet the Lord our God so that we may become the close and near ones before the only begotten Son of God, our Lord Jesus Christ. We ask Him to forgive us our sins, to cover up our errors, and to let us strive to do good in every situation before death visits us. We pray that He spares us from the diabolical temptations, temporal trials and bodily diseases, and make us hear the joyful voice that says, "Come to me, O blessed of my Father, inherit the Kingdom prepared before the foundation of the world, what no eye

has seen, and no ear has heard, and has not entered into the heart of man." [147]

Through the intercession of the Lady of all of us, Theotokos, the immaculate Virgin, mother of light, mother of all, source of grace, the pure Mary, Lady of all creatures and of all martyrs and saints. Now and in all times, until eternity. Amen.

Thus, [we] conclude the life of the holy Abba Moses the Black.

May his prayers be with us. Amen.

Glory to God, always and forever.

---

[147] 1 Corinth. 2:9

CHAPTER SIX
THE SAYINGS OF ABBA MOSES

⁑

⸫ **MOSES 1** – SPIRITUAL WARFARE AGAINST *PORNEIA*[148]

Abba Moses of Petra was terribly embattled by *porneia*. No longer strong enough to remain in his cell he went and reported to Abba Isidore. The elder begged him to return to his cell but he would not accept that, saying, "Abba, I haven't the strength." So he took him and brought him up onto the housetop with him and said to him: "Look to the west." He looked and saw an innumerable host of demons; they were milling around together and shouting, ready for battle. Then Abba Isidore also said to him, "Look to the east." He looked and saw innumerable hosts of glorious holy angels. Then Abba Isidore also said, "Here, these are they who are sent by the Lord to help the holy ones; those in the west are they who are fighting against them. These who are on our side are the more numerous." When he had given thanks to God for this, Abba Moses took courage and returned to his own cell.

⸫ **MOSES 2** – DO NOT JUDGE ANOTHER

A brother once erred at Scetis, and a council was held. They sent for Abba Moses, but he was unwilling to come. So, the priest sent to

---

[148] Moses 1–13 are taken from *Give me a Word*, 193-196 (with some slight revisions to the text).

him, saying, "Come, for the company is waiting for you. He got up and came; he took a basket with many holes, filled it with sand and carried it [with him]. Coming out to meet him, they said to him, "What is this, father?" And the elder said to them, "My sins are running out behind me, and I do not see them—yet here I have come today to pass judgment on the faults of another!" They said nothing to the brother when they heard this, but forgave him.

∴ MOSES 3 – KEEPING SILENT IN GRIEF

Another time there was a council at Scetis. Wanting to put [Abba Moses] to the test, the fathers belittled him, saying, "Why does this Ethiopian come among us too?" But he kept quiet on hearing this. After they were dismissed, they said to him, "Abba, were you not troubled just now?" He said to them, "I was troubled but did not speak" [Ps 76.5].

∴ MOSES 4 – INTERNAL AND EXTERNAL PURITY

They used to say of Abba Moses that when he became a cleric and they put the stole on him, the archbishop said to him, "Look, you have become all white, Abba Moses." The elder said to him, "Maybe outside, my lord Pope, but what about inside?"

∴ **MOSES 4** [CONTINUED] – TESTED BY THE ARCHBISHOP

The bishop wanted to put him to the test; so, he said to the clergy, "When Abba Moses comes into the sanctuary, chase him away and follow him to hear what he says." The elder came in; they denounced him and chased him off, saying, "Get out, Ethiopian." Out he went, saying to himself, "They treated you rightly, ash-skinned black [man]; since you are not human, why come among humans?"

∴ **MOSES 5** – PRACTICAL FASTING

A directive was once issued at Scetis: "Fast this week." It came about that some brothers from Egypt visited Abba Moses and he cooked them a little gruel. Seeing the smoke, his neighbors told the clergy, "Here, Moses has broken the directive of the fathers and cooked himself some gruel." "We ourselves will speak to him when he comes," they said. When Saturday came round, the clergy, well aware of the great discipline of Abba Moses, said to him before the company, "O Abba Moses, you have broken man's law but fulfilled God's."

∴ **MOSES 6** – FINDING TRUE KNOWLEDGE

A brother visited Abba Moses at Scetis asking him for a saying. The elder said to him, "Go and stay in a cell; your cell will teach you everything."

∴ **MOSES 7** – ON SOLITUDE

Abba Moses said, "He who flees from folk is like a bunch of ripe grapes, but he who is among folk is like an unripe grape."

∴ **MOSES 8** – ABBA MOSES HIDES HIS IDENTITY

The governor [of a province] once heard of Abba Moses and off he went to Scetis to see him. When some folk reported the matter to the elder, he got up to run away into the marsh, but they met him and said, "Tell us, elder, where is Abba Moses' cell?" "What do you want from him?" he said to them; "he is crazy!" When the governor came into the church, he said to the clergy, "I am hearing things about Abba Moses and have come to see him and here an elder who was going into Egypt met us. He said to him, "Where is Abba Moses' cell?" and he said to us, "What do you want from him? He is crazy." The clergy were sad when they heard this; they said, "What sort of a person was this elder who said these things against the holy one?" "He was elderly, wearing old clothes, tall and black," they said, and the clergy said, "That is Abba Moses; he said those things so he would not meet you." The governor went his way having reaped great benefit.

⁝ **MOSES 9** – PROPHECY ABOUT THE BARBARIANS

Abba Moses used to say at Scetis, "If we keep the commandments of our fathers, I warrant you in God's name that the barbarians will not be coming here. If we do not keep [them], this place is going to be devastated."

⁝ **MOSES 10** – HIS MARTYRDOM

Once when the brothers were sitting with him, he said to them, "Here the barbarians are coming to Scetis today; but get up and run away!" They said to him, "And you, Abba, are you not running away?" He said to them, "I have been waiting so many years for this day so that the saying of my Lord and master Christ might be fulfilled: 'All who take the sword shall be lost by the sword' [Mt 26.52]." They said to him, "Neither will we run away; we will die with you," but he said to them, "I have nothing to do with that; let each one decide for himself." There were seven brothers and he said to them, "Here are the barbarians, approaching the gate." In they came and killed them, but one of them fled behind some cord for fear and he saw seven crowns descending and crowning them.

∴ **MOSES 11** – BECOME LIKE THE DEAD
A brother asked Abba Moses, "I see something before me and am not able to grasp it." The elder said to him, "Unless you become dead like those in graves you will not be able to grasp it."

∴ **MOSES 12** – NOT TO BE AFFECTED BY EVIL
Abba Poemen said that a brother asked Abba Moses, "In what way does a person make himself dead with respect to his neighbor?" The elder said to him, "Unless a person put it in his heart that he has already been three days in a tomb, he cannot attain to this saying.

∴ **MOSES 13** – MOSES PRAYS TO BE HOSPITABLE
They used to say of Abba Moses at Scetis that when he was about to arrive at Petra, he had exhausted himself travelling there and that he was saying to himself, "How can I collect my water here?" A voice came to him saying, "Come in and do not worry about anything," so in he went. Then some of the fathers visited him and he had only one small vessel of water; while he was boiling a few lentils it was used up. The elder was distressed so, while going in and out, he was praying to God and here a rain-cloud came over Petra itself and he filled all his vessels. After that they said to the elder, "Tell us why you were coming in and going out." The elder said to them, "I was pleading my cause before God, saying, "You brought me hither and here I have no water so that your servants can drink, and that is why

I was coming in and going out, beseeching God until he sent us [water]."

∴ **MOSES 14** – LESSON ON HUMILITY[149]

When a certain brother in Scetis was going to the harvest, he went to Abba Moses the Ethiopian and said to him, "Father, tell me what I shall do; shall I go to the harvest?" and Abba Moses said to him, "If I tell you, will you be persuaded to do as I say?" And the brother said to him, "Yes, I will hearken to you." The elder said to him, "If you will be persuaded by me, rise up, go, and release yourself from going to the harvest, and come unto me, and I will tell you what you shall do." The brother therefore departed and obtained his release from his companions, as the elder had told him, and then he came to him. And the elder said to him, "Go into your cell and keep Pentecost, and you shall eat dry bread and salt once a day, and after you have done this, I will tell you something else to do later on." And he went and did as the elder had told him, and then came to him again. Now when the elder saw that he was one who worked with his hands, he showed him the proper way to live in his cell; and the brother went to his cell, and fell on his face upon the ground, and for three whole days and nights he wept before God. And after these things, when his thoughts were saying to him, "You are now an exalted person, and you have become a great man," he used to contradict them, and

---

[149] Budge, 7 (18).

set before his eyes his former shortcomings and say, "Thus were all your offenses." And again, when they used to say to him, "You have performed many things negligently," he would say, "Nevertheless I do small services for God, and He shows His mercy upon me." And when by such means as these the spirits had been overcome, they appeared to him in the form of corporeal creatures, and said to him, "We have been vanquished by you"; and he said to them, "Why?" and they said to him, "If we humble you, we are raised up by you to an exalted position, and if we exalt you we are accounted by you for humility."

∴ MOSES 15 – PROVERB ON DETERMINATION[150]
Abba Moses used to say, "Secret withdrawal from work makes the mind dark, but for a man to endure and persevere in his works makes light the mind in our Lord, and it strengthens and fortifies the soul."

∴ MOSES 16 – CLOSENESS TO JESUS[151]
Abba Moses said, "He who is very close to Jesus and interrelates with him does well not to bring anybody into his cell."

---

[150] Budge, 50 (227).
[151] *More Anons.*, 549 (N. 703/2.31).

∴ MOSES 17 – LOOK TO YOURSELF[152]

He also said, "It is written that when the Lord killed the firstborn of the Egyptians, there was no house without a dead person."[153] They asked him, "What does this mean?" The elder replied, "If we know that we are all sinners, let us be careful not to ignore our sins and condemn the sins of our neighbor. Indeed, this is ignorant, and it is like the person who has a corpse in his house, and he leaves it and goes to cry over his neighbor's dead. Look at your sins first. Remove your concern in other people, do not come near them, and do not think evil of another. Do not walk with gossipers, and do not believe the words of gossip about another person."

∴ ISAIAH 16 (1) – SPIRITUAL COUNSEL[154]

[Moses] also said, "He who endures injustice for the sake of the Lord is considered a martyr. Whoever adheres for the sake of the Lord, the Lord will sustain him. Whoever remains ignorant for the sake of the Lord will be judged by the Lord."

---

[152] *Bustān*, 101 (183).
[153] Cf. Exod. 11–13
[154] *Bustān*, 101 (184).

∴ ISAIAH 16 (2) – SPIRITUAL COUNSEL[155]

And also, from the sayings of Abba Moses which he sent to Abba *Nūmīn*, by his request: "I prefer your salvation with the fear of God above all things, praying that He make you perfect by His good will so that your toil is not in vain; rather, that it is acceptable to God that you may rejoice. For we find that the merchant, if his trade is profitable, becomes overjoyed. Likewise is the one who learns a craft and becomes overjoyed when he has mastered its skill. He forgets the fatigue that afflicted him because he has mastered the workmanship he so desired. Whoever marries a chaste and self-preserving woman, rejoices in his heart. Whoever receives the honor of soldiership, would go so far as to despise dying in war against the enemies of his kingdom in order to please his master. Every one of those people rejoices when they recognize the goal for which they labored. If this is to be the case in this mortal world, then how much joy is there for the soul that has begun the service of God and completes it according to God's pleasure? Truly, I tell you that the soul's delight will be great. For at the hour of its departure from the world, its deeds will meet it and the angels will rejoice when they see the soul coming home safely, unharmed from the powers of darkness. For when the soul leaves its body, the angels accompany it, but dark powers contend with the soul and prevent it from advancing, seeking to find a fault. When this happens, the angels are

---

[155] *Bustān*, 101-2 (185); *Abbé Isaïe*, s. 16:1–4.

not in the business of fighting for the soul, but the deeds that one had performed are those that protect the soul and keep it from the evil powers. When the soul is victorious by its deeds, the angels will rejoice and glorify God together until it meets the Lord with pleasure. At that hour, the soul will forget all the hardships that have befallen it in this world."

∴ **ISAIAH 16 (3)** – SPIRITUAL COUNSEL[156]

"Our path, O beloved, is to do our utmost and strive with all our strength in this short time to correct our deeds and purify them from all evils, so that we may be saved by the grace of God from the hands of the demons who are eager to meet us. These demons wait for us and hunt for any fault in our deeds because they are evil and have no mercy. So blessed is every soul in which the demons have no place, for it rejoices with great joy. Therefore, O beloved, we should strive as much as we can with tears before our Lord to have mercy on us by His compassion. For those who sow with tears will reap in joy. Let us cherish for ourselves a longing for God. For longing for Him will protect us from fornication. Let us love meekness to be saved from the love of silver. Let us love peace to be saved from hatred. Let us cherish patience and longsuffering because that will protect us from a shrinking soul. Let us love all with pure love, to be rid of jealousy and envy. Let us be humble in every matter and in every work. Let

---

[156] *Bustān*, 102-3 (185 cont.); *Abbé Isaïe*, s. 16:5-20.

us bear insults and defamation to be rid of pride. Let us honor our relatives in all matters that we may be delivered from judgement. Let us reject the esteem and honor of this world that we may be saved from vain glory. Let us use our tongue to commemorate God and for justice to do away with lying. Let us love the purity of heart and body to be delivered from filth. All of this surrounds the soul and follows it when it leaves the body. So whoever is wise and acts wisely, should not surrender their trust without good deeds so that he can be saved from that hardship. Let us be careful as much as we can, and the Lord will help us in our weakness. He knows that humanity is wretched and thus granted them repentance as long as they are in the body."

∴ **ISAIAH 16 (4)** – SPIRITUAL COUNSEL[157]

"Do not worry about the affairs of the world as if they are the goal of our hope in this life, that you may be saved. Have no hope in this world, lest your hope in the Lord weaken. Hate worldly speech so that you may be able to see God with your heart. Pray at all times that you may enlighten your heart with the Lord. Do not be idle, lest you grieve. Tire your body, lest you be condemned in the resurrection of the righteous. Guard your tongue so that the fear of God may dwell in your heart. Give to the needy with pleasure and contentment, lest you be ashamed among the saints and deprived of

---

[157] *Bustān*, 103 (185 cont.); *Abbé Isaïe*, s. 16:21–33.

their glories. Hate the lust of the belly, lest you become surrounded by the Amalekites.[158] Be vigilant in your prayers, lest hidden beasts devour you. Do not love wine, lest it deprive you of the Lord's pleasure. Love the poor so that you may be saved because of them in times of distress. Always commemorate the lives of the saints, so that you are not consumed by the jealousy of their deeds. Remember the Kingdom of Heaven that its desire may move within you. Think of the fire of hell in order to abhor its deeds."

∴ ISAIAH 16 (5) – SPIRITUAL COUNSEL[159]

"If you get up every day in the morning, remember that you will give an answer to God for all your deeds, so do not sin under any circumstance, rather have the fear of God dwell in you. Prepare yourself to meet the Lord and act according to His will. Examine yourself in this place, and know what you lack, so that you may be saved from hardship at the hour of death. Your brothers will see your deeds, and they will be seized by a righteous zeal. Test yourself every day and reflect on every battle you have endured. Do not trust

---

[158] The Amalekites are considered the enemies of God's children and a symbol of evil. Evagrius (345–399) said: "'Amalek was the first of the nations' (Num. 24:20); and gluttony is the first of the passions." See Evagrius of Pontus, "On the Eight Thoughts," in *Evagrius of Pontus: The Greek Ascetic Corpus*, trans. Robert E. Sinkewicz (Oxford University Press, 2003): 73. For the perception of the Church Fathers on Amalek and the Amalekites, see: Mieczysław Celestyn Paczkowski, "Amalek and the Amalekites in the Ancient Christian Literature" in *Teologia Cztowiek 26.2* (Nicolaus Copernicus University: Toruń, 2014): 137–160.

[159] *Bustān*, 103–104 (185 cont.); *Abbé Isaïe*, s. 16:34–49.

yourself but say, 'Mercy and help are from God.' Do not think that you have found anything righteous about yourself until the last breath of your life. Do not be arrogant and say, 'Blessed is me,' because you can never be certain of your enemy's intentions. Do not trust yourself as long as you are in the flesh until the powers of darkness are overcome. Let your heart be very courageous when facing *logismoi*, so that their intensity will be softened. As for the one who is afraid of it, because it frightens him, he in turn becomes proud. Just as the one who is afraid of [*logismoi*] shows that he does not truly believe in God, and cannot pray before Jesus his Master, with all his heart, unless he controls the *logismoi* first. He who desires the dignity of the Lord must be devoted to the purification of the soul from filth. If we think we are blameless, it is because of this that we are defeated. Whoever denies oneself and does not think of themselves as anything, becomes unblemished according to the will of God. Whoever is accustomed to speaking in church has indicated that he does not have the fear of God. This is because the fear of God is preservation and care for the mind, just as the king is a helper to those who obey him. As for those who want to acquire righteousness and have the fear of God in them, if they stumble, they do not despair, rather quickly rise from their fall and are more enthusiastic and focused on good deeds. The most important weapon of the virtues is to fatigue the body by knowledge, for laziness and indulgences breed warfare. He who has knowledge and prudence has defeated evil, for it is written that attention accompanies a wise man, and the weak-willed do not yet know salvation. As for the one who conquers his enemies, he is crowned in the presence of the king."[160]

∴ **ISAIAH 16 (6)** – SPIRITUAL COUNSEL[161]

"If it were not for battles and struggles, there would not be virtue. He who strives with knowledge will be saved from judgment. For [virtue] is the fortified wall. As for the one who condemns, he demolishes his own wall due to a lack of knowledge. Whoever cares to tame his tongue reveals that he is a lover of virtue. And the failure to control the tongue indicates that the inside of the person is devoid of any good deeds. Charity with knowledge gives birth to contemplation of what is to come and leads one to glory. The hard-hearted indicates his lack of any virtue. Freedom births chastity, and the torment of worries brings *logismoi*. Hardness of heart generates anger, and meekness causes mercy. Asceticism of the soul is hatred of luxury, and asceticism of the body is impoverishment. The downfall of the soul is the torment from worries, and its discipline is silence with knowledge. Indulging in sleep arouses the *logismoi*, but salvation of the heart is constant vigil. Too much sleep stirs the imagination but keeping a vigil with knowledge makes the mind blossom and fruitful. Too much sleep swells and darkens the mind,

---

[160] Cf. Prov. 1:2, 2:2, 4:1 and 19:20.
[161] *Bustān*, 104–105 (185 cont.); *Abbé Isaïe*, s. 16:50–62.

but keeping vigil softens and illuminates the mind. He who sleeps with knowledge is better than he who stays awake in vain speech."

∴ ISAIAH 16 (7) – SPIRITUAL COUNSEL[162]

"Mourning expels all kinds of evil when it erupts. If a person accepts reproach and admonishment, then this births humility. As for glorifying people, this births extravagance and egotism. The love of flattery drives out knowledge. Controlling the lust of the stomach reduces the effects of cravings. The lust for food awakens impulses and agitations, but abstaining from them suppresses those feelings. The adornment of the body defeats the soul, and whoever cares about it lacks the fear of God. Remembrance of judgment births the strength of God in the *logismoi*. Lacking the fear of God leads to the mind's deception. Silence with knowledge disciplines the *logismoi*, and a lot of talking generates boredom and obsessiveness. Conquering lust indicates the perfection of virtue, and being defeated by it indicates a lack of knowledge. Persevering in the fear of God protects the soul from warfare, while conversations with the people of the world and mingling with them darkens the soul and makes it forgetful of contemplation."

---

[162] *Bustān*, 105 (185 cont.); *Abbé Isaïe*, s. 16:63–74.

∴ **ISAIAH 16 (8)** – SPIRITUAL COUNSEL[163]

"The love of possessions disturbs the mind, and asceticism gives it enlightenment. The safeguarding of a person is to confess his thoughts; whoever conceals them holds them against himself, but whoever acknowledges them has cast them away from him. It is like a house that has no door or locks, everyone can enter, so is the person who does not control his tongue. And as rust eats through iron, so too does the praise of people spoil the heart if it spreads. And just as ivy wraps around a vineyard and spoils its fruit, so too does vain praise spoil the monk's growth if there are many people around him. As the termite does to wood, so vice does to the soul. The humility of the heart takes precedence over all virtues, and the lust of the stomach is the basis of all suffering. Pride is the root of all evil, and love is the source of all goodness. The worst of all vices is for a person to believe his intelligence is his own. He who denies himself walks in peace. And he who believes in himself, that he is without a defect, is home to all defects. The one who mingles his speech with the speech of worldly people disturbs his heart. The one who neglects the chastity of his body becomes ashamed in his prayers. Loving the people of the world darkens the soul, but distancing from them increases knowledge. The love of toil is a great help, and the root of perdition is laziness."

---

[163] *Bustān*, 105–106 (185 cont.); *Abbé Isaïe*, s. 16:75–87.

∴ ISAIAH 16 (9) – SPIRITUAL COUNSEL[164]

"Protect your eyes, lest your heart be filled with hidden illusions. Whoever looks at a woman with pleasure has committed debauchery with her. Dare not to hear about the fall of one of your brothers, lest you condemn him secretly. Guard your hearing, lest you gather sorrow within yourself. It is better for you to work with your hands so that the poor may take bread from you, because being without a labor is death and collapse of the soul. Persistent prayer is protection from captivity, and whoever delays a little has been cursed by sin."

∴ ISAIAH 16 (10) – SPIRITUAL COUNSEL[165]

"He who remembers his sins and confesses them does not sin much. As for the one who does not remember his sins and acknowledge them, he will be destroyed by them. He who admits his weakness, rebuking himself before God, has taken care to purify his ways from sin. As for the one who delays and says, 'Leave it for another time,' then he becomes a harbor for all malice and deceit. Do not be hard-hearted towards your brother, for we are all overcome by evil thoughts. If you live with the brethren, do not order them to do anything, but work hard with them so that your reward is not lost. If

---

[164] *Bustān*, 106 (185 cont.); *Abbé Isaïe*, s. 16:88–96.
[165] *Bustān*, 106–107 (185 cont.); *Abbé Isaïe*, s. 16:97–114.

the demons wage war against you with food, drinks, and clothing, reject all that they offer. Show them its wretchedness, and they will leave you alone. And if fornication seems good to you, then eradicate it with humility, and turn to God and you will find rest. If you are confronted with the beauty of one's body, then remember its stench after death, and you will find rest. And if thoughts about women entice you, remember the destination of the women of old. Where is their bliss and beauty? All these things do humanity experience by discernment and discretion. Discernment will not come to us unless we recognize the reasons for the onset of evil against us, and this is accomplished by the silence that abounds a monk. Silence begets asceticism, asceticism begets tears, tears beget fear, fear begets humility, and humility is the source of contemplation of what is to be. After receiving sight, love is birthed, and love brings forth health for the soul, free from sicknesses and diseases. By this, man knows that he is not far from God, and so prepares himself for death. He who wants to understand all these dignities should mind their own business and not condemn another. Whenever he prays, the things that bring him closer to God are revealed to him, and he seeks them from Him. He hates this world, for the grace of God grants him all goodness."

∴ ISAIAH 16 (11) – SPIRITUAL COUNSEL[166]

"Therefore, know for certain that every person who eats and drinks without control and loves the vanities of this world cannot obtain anything that is righteous, and indeed he will not realize it, but he deceives himself. If you decide to repent to God, then beware of luxury, for it raises all passions and expels the fear of God from the heart. Seek the fear of God with all your might, for it removes all sins. Do not love comfort as long as you are in this world. Do not trust the body if you ever see yourself resting from warfare at any given time. For passions may suddenly erupt deceitfully and deviously, hoping that a person will refrain from being watchful and cautious. The enemies will strike and abduct the mischievous soul. Therefore, our Lord warns us, saying, 'Be watchful!' Glory be to Him forever and ever. Amen."

∴ ISAIAH 7 – SPIRITUAL COUNSEL[167]

[Moses] also on virtues and vices: "The fear of God expels all vices, and boredom expels the fear of God. These four must be possessed: mercy, the defeat of anger, patience of spirit, and preservation from forgetfulness. At all times, the mind needs these four virtues: persistent prayer with the prostration of heart, combatting *logismoi*, deeming oneself to be a sinner, and never condemning another

---

[166] *Bustān*, 107 (185 cont.); *Abbé Isaïe*, s. 16:115–118.
[167] *Bustān*, 107-108 (186.); *Abbé Isaïe*, s. 7:15–24.

person. These four virtues are an aid for young monks: rumination every hour in the law of God, observing vigils, being active in prayer, considering oneself nothing. Among those things that defile the soul and body are six things: roaming the cities, neglecting the eyes by not protecting them, being acquainted with women, befriending those with authority, loving carnal conversations, and vain speech. These four leads to adultery: eating and drinking, indulging in sleep and idleness, mucking around, and caring for clothing. These four are the source of a darkened mind: hatred of a friend, contempt for them, envy of them, and mistrust of them. By these four things does anger stir in a person: taking and giving, fulfilling desires, a love for teaching others, and thinking that he is intelligent. These four are gained with difficulty: tears, contemplating one's sins, having death at the forefront of their eyes, and to say in every matter, 'I have sinned, forgive me.' He who tills and labors will be saved by the grace of our Lord Jesus Christ."

∴ **ARSENIUS 38** – ABBA ARSENIUS MEETS ABBA MOSES[168]

They used to say of one brother who came to see Abba Arsenius at Scete that he came into church and besought the clergy [that he might] meet with Abba Arsenius. They said to him, "Take a little refreshment brother, and you shall see him," but he said, "I am not

---

[168] *Give me a Word*, Arsenius 38, 50–51.

tasting anything until I meet with him." So they sent a brother to go with him because the elder's cell was far away. They knocked at the door and went in; when they had greeted the elder, they sat in silence. So the brother, the one from the church, said, "I am going [back]; pray for me." Since the brother from elsewhere was not having any communication with the elder, he said to the brother, "I am coming with you too," and out they went together. Then he begged him, "Take me to Abba Moses too, the one who was a brigand." They came to him, and he received them joyfully. He treated them with honor and sent them on their way. Then the brother who was guiding him said, "Here I have taken you to the outsider and to the Egyptian; which of the two pleased you?" In reply he said, "The Egyptian pleased me so far." On hearing this, one of the fathers prayed to God, "Lord, show me this matter: one person avoids people in your name while another welcomes them with open arms in your name," and here there was shown to him two great boats on the river. In one of them he saw Abba Arsenius with the Holy Spirit sailing in *hesychia*, while in the other there sailed Abba Moses and the angels of God and they were feeding him honeycombs.

∴ ZACHARIAH 2 – ON ABBA MOSES[169]

Abba Moses once went to draw some water; he found Abba Zachariah praying by the well and the Spirit of God was resting over him.

∴ ZACHARIAH 3 – TO BE A MONK[170]

Abba Moses once said to Brother Zachariah, "Tell me what I am to do." He threw himself on the ground at the other's feet when he heard this, saying, "You are asking me, father?" The elder said to him, "Believe me, Zachariah my son, I saw the Holy Spirit descending on you, therefore I am obliged to ask you." Then Zachariah took his own cowl from his head, put it beneath his feet and trod on it, saying, "Unless a person be crushed like that, he cannot be a monk."

∴ ZACHARIAH 5 – DEATH OF ABBA ZACHARIAH[171]

Abba Poemen said that Abba Moses asked Brother Zachariah when he was at the point of death, "What do you see?" and he said to him, "Is it not better to keep silent, father?" "It is, my son; be silent," [the elder] said to him. At the moment of his death, Abba Isidore (who was sitting there) looked up to heaven and said, "Rejoice Zachariah

---

[169] *Give me a Word,* Zachariah 2, 110.

[170] *Give me a Word,* Zachariah 3, 110.

[171] *Give me a Word,* Zachariah 5, 110.

my son, for the gates of the Kingdom of Heaven have been opened for you."

∴ ZACHARIAH 6 – DEAD LIKE THE CLOAK[172]
Abba Moses besought Abba Zechariah, saying, "Speak a word of consolation to the brethren", and Zachariah took his cloak, and placed it under his feet saying, "Unless a man die thus, he cannot be a monk."

∴ MACARIUS THE EGYPTIAN 22 – FINDING PEACE[173]
Abba Moses said to Abba Macarius at Scetis, "I wish to live in *hesychia* but the brothers will not let me." Abba Macarius said to him, "I see that yours is a tender nature, and you cannot turn a brother away. But if you wish to live in *hesychia*, go off to the inner desert, to Petra, and live in *hesychia* there." This he did, and experienced repose.

∴ POEMAN 67 – WHOM DO THE DEMONS FIGHT?[174]
Abraham, Abba Agathon's abba, questioned Abba Poemen, "Why are the demons doing battle with me so?" and Abba Poemen said to him, "Are the demons doing battle with you? The demons do not

---
[172] Budge, 13 (40). Given a new numbering.
[173] *Give me a Word*, Macarius the Egyptian 22, 186–187.
[174] *Give me a Word*, Poemen 67, 238.

battle with us as long as we are following our own wills, for our wills have become demons; it is they that oppress us so that we fulfill them. Do you want to see with whom the demons do battle? It is with Moses and those like him."

∴ **POEMAN 165** – ERA OF MOSES[175]
Abba Poemen said, "Since Abba Moses and the third generation in Scetis, the brothers do not make progress anymore."

∴ **SILVANUS 11** – NEW BEGINNINGS[176]
Abba Moses asked Abba Silvanus, "Can a man lay a new foundation every day?" The elder said, "If he works hard, he can lay a new foundation at every moment."

∴ **AN ELDER 1** – ON DEFEATING PASSIONS[177]
The brethren said, "Why is it that though the holy fathers incite us continually to the labors of excellence, and to the contending against passions and devils, Abba Isidore restrained Abba Moses the Ethiopian from works, and from contests with devils, saying, 'Rest, O Moses, and quarrel not with the devils, and seek not to make attacks upon them, for there is a measure [i.e., moderation] in

---

[175] *Give me a Word*, Poemen 165, 254.
[176] *Give me a Word*, Silvanus 11, 294.
[177] Budge, 289–290 (617).

everything.' Does this apply also to works and to the labors of the ascetic life?"

The elder said, "Because at the beginning Abba Moses was ignorant of the rule of the ascetic life, and because he was healthy of body, he worked overmuch, and he thought that he would be able to prevail mightily against devils by the multitude of his works alone, and that he would be able to vanquish them. Therefore, because the devils perceived his object, they attacked him more severely with frequent wars, both secretly and openly. But Abba Isidore, wishing to teach him the truth, and to make him acquire humility, said to him, 'Without the power of the Spirit which our Lord gave us in baptism for the fulfilling of His commandments, which is confirmed in us each day by the taking of His Body and Blood, we cannot be purified from the passions, and we cannot vanquish devils, and we cannot perform the works of spiritual excellence.' Thereupon Abba Moses learned these things, and his thoughts were humbled, and he partook of the Holy Mysteries. The devils were conquered, and they reduced their war against him, and from that time forward he lived in rest, and knowledge and peace. Many monks have imagined that their passions would be healed, and that they would acquire soundness of soul merely by their labors and strenuousness, and therefore they were abandoned by grace, and fell from the truth. For as he who is sick in his body cannot be healed without the physician and medicines, however much he may watch and fast during the time he is taking the medicine, so he who is sick in his soul through the passions of sin, without Christ, the Physician of souls, and without partaking of His Body and Blood, and the power which is hidden in His commandments, and the humility which is like unto His, cannot be healed of his passions, and cannot receive a perfect cure. Therefore, whoever fights against passions and the devils by the commandments of our Lord is healed of the sicknesses of the passions and acquires health of soul and is delivered from the crafts of the devil."

∴ **AN ELDER 2** – ON DIVINE GRACE'S CALLING[178]

The brethren said, "In how many ways does Divine Grace call the brethren to the life of the solitary ascetic?" The elder said, "In very many and different ways. Sometimes Divine Grace moves a man suddenly, even as it moved Abba Moses the Ethiopian, and sometimes by the hearing of Scriptures, as in the cases of the blessed Abba Antony and Abba Simon Stylites, and others by the doctrine of the word, as in the cases of Serapion, and Abba Bessarion, and others who were like them. Concerning these three ways, whereby Divine Grace calls to those who repent, I would say that Divine Grace moves the conscience of a monk in the manner which is pleasing to God, and that through these, even evildoers have

---

[178] Budge, 317 (657).

repented and pleased God. And there is moreover, the departure from this world by the hands of angels; by terrors, by sicknesses, and afflictions, even as that which took place in respect of the blessed Evagrius; and sometimes God Himself calls from heaven and takes a man out of the world, as in the cases of Paul and Abba Arsenius."

∴ AN ELDER 3 – ON TAMING ANGER[179]

The brethren said: Abba Moses the Ethiopian was on one occasion reviled by certain men, and the brethren asked him, "Were you not troubled in your heart, O father, when you were reviled?" And he said to them, "Although I was troubled, I said nothing."

"What is the meaning of the words: although I was troubled, I spoke not?" The elder replied, "The perfection of monks consists of two parts, that is to say, of impassibility of the senses of the body, and of impassibility of the senses of the soul. Impassibility of the body takes place when a man who is reviled restrains himself for God's sake and speaks not, even though he is troubled; but impassibility of the soul takes place when a man is abused and reviled, and yet is not angry in his heart when he is abused, even like John Colobos. For on one occasion, when the brethren were sitting with him, a man passed by and upbraided him, but he was not angry, and his countenance did not change. Then the brethren asked him, 'Are you not secretly

---

[179] Budge, 325–326 (669).

troubled in your heart, O father, being reviled in this fashion?' And he answered and said to them, 'I am not troubled inwardly, for inwardly I am just as tranquil as you see that I am outwardly.' And this is what is known as impassibility." Now at that time Abb Moses had not arrived at this state of perfection, and he confessed that although outwardly he was undisturbed, yet he was waging a contest in his heart, and he maintained silence and was not angry outwardly. Even this was a spiritual excellence, although it would have been a more perfect thing had he not been angry either inwardly or outwardly.

The blessed Nilus made a comparison of these two measures of excellence in the cases of the blessed men Moses and Aaron. The act of covering the breast and heart with the priestly tunic which Aaron performed when he went into the Holy of Holies represented the state of a man who, though angry in his heart, suppresses his wrath by struggling and prayer; and the state of a man not being angry at all in the heart, because he has been exalted to perfection by [his] victory over the passions and the devils. Nilus compared that to which is said of the blessed Moses, "Moses took the breast for an offering, because the soul dwells in the heart, and the heart in the breast" [Lev. 8:29]. And Solomon said, "Remove anger from your heart" [Ecc. 11:10], and concerning Aaron the Book said, "He was covering his breast with the ephod and tunic" [Ex. 29:5]. This teaches us monks that it is meet for us to cover over the wrath which is in the heart with gentle, humble, and tranquil thoughts, and that we should not allow it to ascend to the opening of our throat, and that the odiousness and abomination thereof shall be revealed by the tongue.

CHAPTER SEVEN
SEVEN INSTRUCTIONS WHICH ABBA MOSES SENT TO ABBA POEMEN.[180]

HE WHO PUTS THEM INTO PRACTICE WILL ESCAPE ALL PUNISHMENT AND WILL LIVE IN PEACE, WHETHER HE DWELLS IN THE DESERT OR IN THE MIDST OF BRETHREN.

1. The monk must die to his neighbor and never judge him at all, in any way whatsoever.

2. The monk must die to everything before leaving the body, in order not to harm anyone.

3. If the monk does not think in his heart that he is a sinner, God will not hear him. The brother said, "What does that mean, to think in his heart that he is a sinner?" Then the elder said, "When someone is occupied with his own faults, he does not see those of his neighbor."

4. If a man's deeds are not in harmony with his prayer, he labors in vain. The brother said, "What is this harmony between practice and prayer?" The elder said, "We should no longer do those things against which we pray. For when a man gives up his own will, then

---

[180] Ward, *The Sayings of the Desert Fathers*, 141–143

God is reconciled with him and accepts his prayers." The brother asked, "In all the affliction which the monk gives himself, what helps him?" The elder said, "It is written, 'God is our refuge and strength, a very present help in trouble.'" [Ps.46:1]

5. The elder was asked, "What is the good of the fasts and vigils which a man imposes on himself?" and he replied, "They make the soul humble. For it is written, 'Consider my affliction and my trouble, and forgive all my sins' [Ps. 25:18]. So if the soul gives itself all this hardship, God will have mercy on it."

6. The elder was asked, "What should a man do in all the temptations and evil thoughts that come upon him?" The elder said, "He should weep and implore the goodness of God to come to his aid, and he will obtain peace if he prays with discernment. For it is written, 'With the Lord on my side I do not fear. What can man do to me?'" [Ps. 118:6]

7. A brother asked the elder, "Here is a man who beats his servant because of a fault he has committed; what will the servant say?" The elder replied, "If the servant is good, he should say, 'Forgive me, I have sinned.'" The brother said to him, "Nothing else?" The elder said, "No, for from the moment he takes upon himself responsibility for the affair and says, 'I have sinned,' immediately the Lord will have mercy on him. The aim in all these things is not to judge one's neighbor. For truly, when the hand of the Lord caused all the first-

born in the land of Egypt to die, no house was without its dead." The brother said, "What does that mean?" The elder said, "If we are on the watch to see our own faults, we shall not see those of our neighbor. It is folly for a man who has a dead person in his house to leave him there and go to weep over his neighbor's dead. To die to one's neighbor is this: To bear your own faults and not to pay attention to anyone else wondering whether they are good or bad. Do no harm to anyone, do not think anything bad in your heart towards anyone, do not scorn the man who does evil, do not put confidence in him who does wrong to his neighbor, do not rejoice with him who injures his neighbor. This is what dying to one's neighbor means. Do not rail against anyone, but rather say, 'God knows each one.' Do not agree with him who slanders; do not rejoice at his slander and do not hate him who slanders his neighbor. This is what it means not to judge. Do not have hostile feelings towards anyone and do not let dislike dominate your heart; do not hate him who hates his neighbor. This is what peace is. Encourage yourself with this thought, 'Affliction lasts but a short time, while peace is forever, by the grace of God the Word. Amen.'"

CHAPTER EIGHT

DOXOLOGY 1[179]

1	The holy protomartyr ✣ who was well perfected ✣ on the mountain of Scetis ✣ is our holy father Abba Moses.	ⲡⲓϣⲟⲣⲡ ⲙ̄ⲙⲁⲣⲧⲩⲣⲟⲥ ⲉ̄ⲑ︦ⲩ︦ ✣ ⲉ̀ⲧⲁϥϫⲱⲕ ⲉ̀ⲃⲟⲗ ⲛ̀ⲕⲁⲗⲱⲥ ✣ ϧⲉⲛ ⲡⲓⲧⲱⲟⲩ ⲛ̀ⲧⲉ ϣⲓϩⲏⲧ ✣ ⲡⲉ ⲡⲉⲛⲓⲱⲧ ⲉ̄ⲑ︦ⲩ︦ ⲁⲃⲃⲁ ⲙⲱⲥⲏ.
2	He became a fighter ✣ whom the demons feared ✣ he stood upon Petra ✣ as a symbol of the Cross.	ⲁϥϣⲱⲡⲓ ⲅⲁⲣ ⲛ̀ⲟⲩⲣⲉϥϯ ✣ ⲉϥⲟⲓ ⲛ̀ϩⲟϯ ⲟⲩⲃⲉ ⲛⲓⲇⲉⲙⲱⲛ ✣ ⲁϥⲟϩⲓ ⲉ̀ⲣⲁⲧϥ ϩⲓϫⲉⲛ ϯⲡⲉⲧⲣⲁ ✣ ⲕⲁⲧⲁ ⲡ̀ⲧⲩⲡⲟⲥ ⲙ̀ⲡⲓⲥ︦ⲧ︦ⲁⲩⲣⲟⲥ.
3	Through his great endurance ✣ in the toils of his suffering ✣ he bore the crown ✣ of martyrdom.	ϩⲓⲧⲉⲛ ⲧⲉϥⲛⲓϣϯ ⲛ̀ϩⲩⲡⲟⲙⲟⲛⲏ ✣ ⲛⲉⲙ ⲡⲓϩⲓⲥⲓ ⲛ̀ⲧⲉ ⲛⲓⲃⲁⲥⲁⲛⲟⲥ ✣ ⲁϥⲉⲣⲫⲟⲣⲓⲛ ⲙ̀ⲡⲓⲭ̀ⲗⲟⲙ ✣ ⲛ̀ⲧⲉ ϯⲙⲉⲧⲙⲁⲣⲧⲩⲣⲟⲥ.
4	He flew high by the Spirit ✣ to his place of rest ✣ which the Lord has prepared ✣ for	ⲁϥϩⲱⲗ ⲉ̀ⲛ̀ϭⲓⲥⲓ ϧⲉⲛ ⲡⲓⲡ̀ⲛⲉⲩⲙⲁ ✣ ⲉ̀ϧⲟⲩⲛ ⲉ̀ⲛⲉϥⲙⲁⲛⲉⲙⲧⲟⲛ ✣ ⲉ̀ⲧⲁϥⲥⲉⲃⲧⲱⲧⲟⲩ ⲛ̀ϫⲉ ⲡ︦ⲟ︦ⲥ︦ ✣ ⲛ̀ⲛⲏⲉⲑⲙⲉⲓ ⲙ̀ⲡⲉϥⲣⲁⲛ ⲉ̄ⲑ︦ⲩ︦.

---

[179] al-Qummuṣ Mīnā al-Miḥalāwī al-Baramūsī, ⲡⲓϫⲱⲙ ⲛⲧⲉ ϯⲯⲁⲗⲙⲟⲇⲓⲁ ⲉⲑⲟⲩⲁⲃ ⲛⲧⲉⲛⲣⲟⲙⲡⲓ, (Cairo: Monastery of al-Baramūs, reprinted 2017), 573–575.

those who love His holy name.

5. He left for us his holy body ✣ and his holy cave ✣ that we may complete in it ✣ his honored commemoration.

ⲁϥⲥⲱϫⲡ ⲛⲁⲛ ⲙ̀ⲡⲉϥⲥⲱⲙⲁ ✣ ⲛⲉⲙ ⲡⲉϥⲥ̀ⲡⲏⲗⲉⲟⲛ ⲉ̅ⲑ̅ⲩ̅ ✣ ⲉⲑⲣⲉⲛϫⲱⲕ ⲉ̀ⲃⲟⲗ ⲛ̀ϧⲏⲧϥ ✣ ⲙ̀ⲡⲉϥⲉⲣⲫⲙⲉⲩⲓ ⲉⲧⲧⲁⲓⲏ̀ⲟⲩⲧ.

6. Proclaiming and saying ✣ "O God of Abba Moses ✣ and those who were perfected with him ✣ have mercy upon our souls."

ⲉⲛⲱϣ ⲉ̀ⲃⲟⲗ ⲉⲛϫⲱ ⲙ̀ⲙⲟⲥ ✣ ϫⲉ ⲫϯ ⲛ̀ⲁⲃⲃⲁ ⲙⲱⲥⲏ ✣ ⲛⲉⲙ ⲛⲏⲉ̀ⲧⲁⲩϫⲱⲕ ⲉ̀ⲃⲟⲗ ⲛⲉⲙⲁϥ ✣ ⲁ̀ⲣⲓⲟⲩⲛⲁⲓ ⲛⲉⲙ ⲛⲉⲛⲯⲩⲭⲏ.

7. That we may win the promises ✣ which He has prepared for the saints ✣ who have pleased Him since the beginning ✣ because of their love for Him.

ⲟⲩⲟϩ ⲛ̀ⲧⲉⲛϣⲁϣⲛⲓ ⲉ̀ⲛⲓⲱϣ ✣ ⲉ̀ⲧⲁϥⲥⲉⲃⲧⲱⲟⲩ ⲛ̀ⲛⲏⲉ̅ⲑ̅ⲩ̅ ✣ ⲉ̀ⲧⲁⲩⲣⲁⲛⲁϥ ⲓⲥϫⲉⲛ ⲡ̀ⲉⲛⲉϩ ✣ ⲉⲑⲃⲉ ⲧⲟⲩⲁ̀ⲅⲁⲡⲏ ⲉ̀ϧⲟⲩⲛ ⲉ̀ⲣⲟϥ.

8. Pray to the Lord on our behalf ✣ O my master and father Abba Moses ✣ and his children the cross-bearers ✣ that He may forgive us our sins.

ⲧⲱⲃϩ ⲙ̀ⲡ̅ⲟ̅ⲥ̅ ⲉ̀ϩ̀ⲣⲏⲓ ⲉ̀ϫⲱⲛ ✣ ⲱ̀ ⲡⲁⲟ̅ⲥ̅ ⲛ̀ⲓⲱⲧ ⲁⲃⲃⲁ ⲙⲱⲥⲏ ✣ ⲛⲉⲙ ⲛⲉϥϣⲏⲣⲓ ⲛ̀ⲥⲧⲁⲩⲣⲟⲫⲟⲣⲟⲥ ✣ ⲛ̀ⲧⲉϥⲭⲁ ⲛⲉⲛⲛⲟⲃⲓ ⲛⲁⲛ ⲉ̀ⲃⲟⲗ.

Chapter Eight: Hymns

DOXOLOGY 2

IN MS COPTIC MUSEUM 292 (LITURGY 341)[180]

1	Philip the Apostle ☩ baptized the Ethiopian eunuch ☩ of Candace ☩ queen of the Ethiopians.	ⲫⲓⲗⲓⲡⲡⲟⲥ ⲡⲁⲡⲟⲥⲧⲟⲗⲟⲥ ☩ ⲁϥⲧⲱⲙⲥ ⲙ̄ⲡⲓⲉⲑⲱϣ ☩ ⲛ̄ⲥⲓⲟⲩⲣ ⲛ̄ⲧⲉ ⲕⲁⲇⲁⲕⲏⲥ ☩ ϯⲟⲩⲣⲱ ⲛ̄ⲧⲉ ⲛⲓⲉⲑⲁⲩϣ.
2	Our holy father Abba Macarius ☩ and our father Isidore ☩ baptized the Ethiopian ☩ and he became white like snow.	ⲡⲉⲛⲓⲱⲧ ⲉⲑⲟⲩⲁⲃ ⲁⲃⲃⲁ ⲙⲁⲕⲁⲣⲓ ☩ ⲛⲉⲙ ⲡⲉⲛⲓⲱⲧ ⲁⲃⲃⲁ ⲓⲥⲓⲇⲱⲣⲟⲥ ☩ ⲁⲩⲧⲱⲙⲥ ⲙ̄ⲡⲓⲉⲑⲱϣ ☩ ⲁϥⲟⲩⲁϣⲃ̄ ⲙ̄ⲫⲣⲏϯ ⲛ̄ⲟⲩⲭⲓⲟⲛ.
3	He, who was the first among thieves ☩ in the district of Gaza ☩ through	ⲫⲁⲓ ⲉⲛⲁϥⲟⲓ ⲛ̄ⲥⲟⲛⲓ ⲛ̄ϣⲟⲣⲡ ☩ ϧⲉⲛ ⲡⲓⲑⲱϣ ⲛ̄ⲧⲉ ⲅⲁⲍⲁ ☩ ϩⲓⲧⲉⲛ ⲡⲓϩⲁⲗⲏⲧ ⲛ̄ϣⲟⲩⲙⲉⲥⲧⲁϥ ☩ ⲟⲩⲟϩ ⲛ̄ϯⲁⲃⲟⲗⲟⲥ ⲉⲧϩⲱⲟⲩ.

---

[180] This was first printed by Fr Dūmādiyūs al-Baramūsī's 1922 edition ⲛ̄ϫⲱⲙ ⲛ̄ⲧⲉ ⲛⲓϫⲓⲛϯⲱⲟⲩ ⲉⲑⲩ̄ ⲛ̄ϯⲡⲁⲣⲑⲉⲛⲟⲥ ⲛⲓⲁⲅⲅⲉⲗⲟⲥ ⲛⲓⲁⲡⲟⲥⲧⲟⲗⲟⲥ ⲛⲓⲙⲁⲣⲧⲩⲣⲟⲥ ⲛⲉⲙ ⲛⲏⲉⲑⲩ̄ [The book of the holy venerations of the Virgin, angels, apostles, martyrs and saints], (Cairo: 1922), 259–260. Yassa ʿAbd al-Massīḥ documented this doxology in, "Doxologies in the Coptic Church: Unedited Bohairic Doxologies (Tûbah – An- Nâsi)." BSAC 11 (1945):129–130. Prof. Youssef later published this doxology in his article, "Coptic and Arabic Liturgical texts relating to Moses the black", *ΣΥΝΑΞΙΣΚΑΘΟΛΙΚΗ. Beiträge zu Gottesdienst und Geschichte der fünf Patriarchate für Heinzgerd Brakmann zum 70* (2014):751–766. I have revised the English translation.

the most hated bird ✛ and
the wicked devil.

4 He who withdrew ✛ is the victorious martyr ✛ and mighty one of Christ ✛ our holy father Abba Moses.

ⲫⲏⲉⲧⲁϥⲉⲣⲁⲡⲟⲧⲁⲍⲉ ✛ ⲥⲑⲉ ⲙ̀ⲙⲟϥ ⲛ̀ϫⲉ ⲡⲁⲑⲗⲓⲧⲏⲥ ⲙ̀ⲙⲁⲣⲧⲩⲣⲟⲥ ✛ ⲟⲩⲟϩ ⲛ̀ϫⲱⲣⲓ ⲛ̀ⲧⲉ ⲡⲭ̅ⲥ̅ ✛ ⲡⲉⲛⲓⲱⲧ ⲉ̅ⲑ̅ⲩ̅ ⲁⲃⲃⲁ ⲙⲟⲩⲥⲏ.

5 Therefore, he brought ✛ the evil berbers ✛ who killed him and his children ✛ upon the top of Petra.

ⲉⲑⲃⲉ ⲫⲁⲓ ⲁϥⲓⲛⲓ ⲉϫⲱϥ ✛ ⲛ̀ⲛⲓⲃⲁⲣⲃⲁⲣⲟⲥ ⲉⲧϩⲱⲟⲩ ✛ ⲁⲩϧⲱⲧⲉⲃ ⲙ̀ⲙⲟϥ ⲛⲉⲙ ⲛⲉϥϣⲏⲣⲓ ✛ ⲉϩⲣⲏⲓ ⲉϫⲉⲛ ⲧⲁⲫⲉ ⲛ̀ϯⲡⲉⲧⲣⲁ.

6 Pray [to the Lord on our behalf] ✛ my lord and father Abba Moses ✛ and his children the cross-bearers ✛ so that [He may forgive us our sins.]

ⲧⲱⲃϩ [ⲙ̀ⲡ̅ⲟ̅ⲥ̅ ⲉϩⲣⲏⲓ ⲉϫⲱⲛ] ✛ ⲡⲁⲟ̅ⲥ̅ ⲛ̀ⲓⲱⲧ ⲁⲃⲃⲁ ⲙⲟⲩⲥⲏ ✛ ⲛⲉⲙ ⲛⲉϥϣⲏⲣⲓ ⲛ̀ⲥⲧⲁⲩⲣⲟⲫⲱⲣⲟⲥ ✛ ⲛ̀ⲧⲉϥ [ⲭⲁ ⲛⲉⲛⲛⲟⲃⲓ ⲛⲁⲛ ⲉⲃⲟⲗ.]

Chapter Eight: Hymns

PSALI ADAM[181]

1	I want to become ✛ a dove ✛ and fly to the cave ✛ of Abba Moses	ϯoyωϣ ⲛ̄ⲧⲁⲉⲣ ✛ oyϭⲣoⲙⲡⲓ ⲛ̄ⲧⲁϩⲁⲗⲁⲓ ✛ ⲛ̄ⲧⲁϩⲱⲗ ⲡⲓⲥⲡⲏⲗⲉoⲛ ✛ ⲛ̄ⲧⲉ ⲁⲃⲃⲁ ⲙⲱⲩⲥⲏ
2	In order to prostrate ✛ in front of his relics ✛ before they are removed ✛ from the cave	ⲛ̄ⲧⲁoⲩⲱϣⲧ ⲉϩⲣⲏⲓ ⲉϫⲉⲛ ✛ ⲛⲉϥⲗⲩⲯⲁⲛoⲛ ✛ ⲙ̄ⲡⲁⲧoⲩoⲗϥ ✛ ⲉⲃoⲗϧⲉⲛ ⲡⲓⲥⲡⲏⲗⲉoⲛ
3	That I may entreat him ✛ to pray to the Lord ✛ on my behalf ✛ and the sins of my soul	ⲛ̄ⲧⲁϯϩo ⲉⲣoϥ ✛ ⲛ̄ⲧⲉϥⲧⲱⲃϩ ⲙ̄ⲡⲟ̄ⲥ̄ ✛ ⲉϩⲣⲏⲓ ⲉϫⲉⲛ ⲛⲓⲛoⲃⲓ ✛ ⲧⲁⲯⲩⲭⲏ

---

[181] Given the title "Adam Doxology to St. Abba Moses the Black" in Arsānyūs al-Muḥarraqī, ⲡϫⲱⲙ ⲛ̄ⲧⲉ ⲛⲓϫⲓⲛϯⲱoⲩ ⲉⲑ︤ⲩ︥ ⲛ̄ϯⲡⲁⲣⲑⲉⲛoⲥ ⲛⲓⲁⲅⲅⲉⲗoⲥ ⲛⲓⲁⲡoⲥⲧoⲗoⲥ ⲛⲓⲙⲁⲣⲧⲩⲣoⲥ ⲛⲉⲙ ⲛⲏⲉⲑoⲩⲁⲃ [*the book of the holy veneration of the Virgin, angels, apostles, martyrs, and the saints*], (Cairo, 1972), 329–331. This doxology also appears in a parchment in the Monastery of St. Macarius with the appropriate title ⲥoⲩ ⲕ︤ⲇ︥ ⲙ̄ⲡⲓⲁⲱⲛⲓ ϯⲁⲗⲓ ⲛ̄ⲭoⲥ ⲁⲇⲁⲙ [On the 24th of *Ba 'ūna*, a Psali in the Adam Tune], H. G. Evelyn White, *The Monasteries of Wadi 'N Natrûn. Part 1: New Coptic Texts from the Monastery of Saint Macarius*, (New York, 1926), 138. For a brief commentary on this doxology, see Youssef, "Coptic and Arabic Liturgical texts relating to Moses the black," 754.

4	That Christ our God ✛ the compassionate ✛ may forgive my sins ✛ before [my soul] leaves my body	ⲛ̄ⲧⲉϥⲭⲱ ⲛⲏⲓ ⲉⲃⲟⲗ ✛ ⲙ̄ⲡⲁⲧⲉⲥⲓ ⲉⲃⲟⲗϧⲉⲛ ⲡⲁⲥⲱⲙⲁ ✛ ⲛ̄ϫⲉ ⲡⲭ̄ⲥ̄ ⲡⲉⲛⲛⲟⲩϯ ✛ ⲫⲁ ⲛⲓⲙⲉⲧϣⲉⲛϩⲏⲧ
5	In order to find ✛ mercy and courage ✛ before Him ✛ in His Kingdom	ⲛ̄ⲧⲁϫⲓⲙⲓ ⲛ̄ⲟⲩⲛⲁⲓ ✛ ⲙ̄ⲡⲉϥⲙ̄ⲑⲟ ⲉⲃⲟⲗ ✛ ⲛⲉⲙ ⲟⲩⲡⲁⲣⲣⲏⲥⲓⲁ ✛ ϧⲉⲛ ⲧⲉϥⲙⲉⲧⲟⲩⲣⲟ
6	Through [the prayers] of our father ✛ Abba Moses ✛ O Lord, grant us ✛ the forgiveness of our sins.	ϩⲓⲧⲉⲛ [ⲛⲓⲉⲩⲭⲏ] ⲛ̄ⲧⲉ ⲡⲉⲛⲓⲱⲧ ✛ ⲁⲃⲃⲁ ⲙⲟⲩⲥⲏ ✛ ⲙ̄ⲡ̄ⲟ̄ⲥ̄ ⲁⲣⲓϩⲙⲟⲧ ⲛⲁⲛ ✛ ⲙ̄ⲡⲓⲭⲱ ⲉⲃⲟⲗ ⲛ̄ⲧⲉ ⲛⲉⲛⲛⲟⲃⲓ

PSALI WATOS[182]

1	Come all you faithful ⁘ to worship Jesus Christ ⁘ and to honor the blessed one ⁘ O strong saint, Abba Moses!	ⲁⲙⲱⲓⲛⲓ ⲧⲏⲣⲟⲩ ⲱ̄ ⲛⲓⲡⲓⲥⲧⲟⲥ ⁘ ⲛ̄ⲧⲉⲛⲟⲩⲱϣⲧ ⲛ̄ⲓⲏ̄ⲥ ⲡⲭ̄ⲥ̄ ⁘ ⲛ̄ⲧⲉⲛⲧⲁⲓⲟ ⲙ̄ⲡⲓⲙⲁⲕⲁⲣⲓⲟⲥ ⁘ ⲡⲓϫⲱⲣⲓ ⲉ̄ⲟ̄ⲩ̄ ⲁⲃⲃⲁ ⲙⲱⲥⲏ.
2	Everyone in all places ⁘ is honored by this life ⁘ of the protomartyr ⁘ O strong saint, Abba Moses!	ⲃⲟⲛ ⲛⲓⲃⲉⲛ ϧⲉⲛ ⲙⲁⲓ ⲛⲓⲃⲉⲛ ⁘ ϥ̄ⲧⲛⲓⲁⲧϥ ⲙ̄ⲡⲁⲓⲃⲓⲟⲥ ⲫⲁⲓ ⁘ ⲛ̄ⲧⲉ ⲡⲓϣⲱⲣⲡ ⲙ̄ⲙⲁⲣⲧⲩⲣⲟⲥ ⁘ ⲡⲓϫⲱⲣⲓ ⲉ̄ⲟ̄ⲩ̄ ⲁⲃⲃⲁ ⲙⲱⲥⲏ.
3	All the Christian people ⁘ praising God with psalms ⁘ on the feast of our saint ⁘ O strong saint, Abba Moses!	ⲅⲉⲛⲟⲥ ⲛ̄ⲛⲓⲭⲣⲓⲥⲧⲓⲁⲛⲟⲥ ⁘ ⲉⲩϩⲱⲥ ⲉ̄ⲫϯ ϧⲉⲛ ϩⲁⲛⲯⲁⲗⲙⲟⲥ ⁘ ϩⲛ ⲡϣⲁⲓ ⲙ̄ⲡⲉⲛⲁⲅⲓⲟⲥ ⁘ ⲡⲓϫⲱⲣⲓ ⲉ̄ⲟ̄ⲩ̄ ⲁⲃⲃⲁ ⲙⲱⲥⲏ.
4	Come, O David, in our midst today ⁘ to praise this honorable martyr ⁘ of the	ⲇⲁⲩⲓⲇ ⲁⲙⲟⲩ ⲧⲉⲛⲙⲏϯ ⲙ̄ⲫⲟⲟⲩ ⁘ ⲛ̄ⲧⲉⲕϫⲱ ⲙ̄ⲡ̄ⲧⲁⲓⲟ ⲙ̄ⲡⲁⲓⲙⲁⲣⲩⲣⲟⲥ ⁘ ⲛ̄ⲧⲉ ⲡⲟⲩⲣⲟ ⲛ̄ⲧⲉ ⲡⲱⲟⲩ ⁘ ⲡⲓϫⲱⲣⲓ ⲉ̄ⲟ̄ⲩ̄ ⲁⲃⲃⲁ ⲙⲱⲥⲏ.

---

[182] This Psali Watos is taken from Coptic Reader as I could not find it in Fr Fīlūtā'us al-Maqqārī, *Kitāb al-Ibṣāliyāt w-al-Ṭurūḥāt al-Wāṭuṣ w-al-Adām vol. 1* (Cairo: 1913), nor in its continuing edition by al-Anbā Mattāūs w-al-Anbā Ṣamū'īl, *al-Ibṣāliyāt w-al-Wāṭuṣ w-al-Adām. Baramhāt - al-Šhahr al-Ṣaġīr vol. 2* (Cairo: 1994).

	King of glory ✢ O strong saint, Abba Moses!	
5	Through mercy ✢ this struggler was saved ✢ through suffering and perseverance ✢ O strong saint, Abba Moses!	ⲉⲃⲟⲗ ϩⲓⲧⲉⲛ ϯⲙⲉⲑⲛⲁϩⲧ ✢ ⲁϥⲛⲟϩⲉⲙ ⲛ̀ϫⲉ ⲡⲁⲓⲁⲑⲗⲓⲧⲏⲥ ✢ ϩⲁⲛⲙⲉⲧϣⲱϫ ⲛⲉⲙ ϩⲁⲛϣ̀ⲣⲱⲓⲥ ✢ ⲡⲓϫⲱⲣⲓ ⲉ̅ⲑ̅ⲩ̅ ⲁⲃⲃⲁ ⲙⲱⲥⲏ.
6	Many are your wonders ✢ performed in your monastery ✢ everywhere and in every place ✢ O strong saint, Abba Moses!	ⲍⲉⲟϣ ⲛ̀ϫⲉ ⲛⲉⲕϣ̀ⲫⲏⲣⲓ ✢ ⲛⲏⲉⲧⲁⲕⲁⲓⲧⲟⲩ ϧⲉⲛ ⲡⲉⲕⲁⲃⲏⲧ ✢ ⲛⲉⲙ ⲧⲟⲡⲟⲥ ⲛⲓⲃⲉⲛ ⲛⲉⲙ ⲙⲁⲓ ⲛⲓⲃⲉⲛ ✢ ⲡⲓϫⲱⲣⲓ ⲁⲃⲃⲁ ⲉ̅ⲑ̅ⲩ̅ ⲙⲱⲥⲏ.
7	Isidore the longsuffering ✢ accepted him with kindness ✢ and led him to the path ✢ O strong saint, Abba Moses!	ⲏⲥⲓⲇⲱⲣⲟⲥ ⲡⲓⲣⲉϥϣⲟⲩⲛ̀ϩⲏⲧ ✢ ⲁϥϣⲟⲡϥ ⲉⲣⲟϥ ϧⲉⲛ ⲟⲩⲙⲉⲑⲛⲁϩⲧ ✢ ⲁϥⲉⲣⲥⲩⲙⲙⲉⲛⲓⲛ ⲛⲁϥ ⲙ̀ⲡⲓⲙⲱⲓⲧ ✢ ⲡⲓϫⲱⲣⲓ ⲉ̅ⲑ̅ⲩ̅ ⲁⲃⲃⲁ ⲙⲱⲥⲏ.
8	Gather all of my senses ✢ and the thoughts of my heart ✢ to honor the martyr ✢ O strong saint, Abba Moses!	ⲑⲱⲟⲩϯ ϩⲁⲣⲟⲓ ⲱ̀ ⲛⲁⲗⲟⲅⲓⲥⲙⲟⲥ ✢ ⲛⲉⲙ ⲛⲁⲙⲉⲩⲓ ⲉϧⲟⲩⲛ ⲉⲡⲁϩⲏⲧ ✢ ⲛ̀ⲧⲁⲧⲓⲟ ⲙ̀ⲡⲓⲙⲁⲣⲧⲩⲣⲟⲥ ✢ ⲡⲓϫⲱⲣⲓ ⲉ̅ⲑ̅ⲩ̅ ⲁⲃⲃⲁ ⲙⲱⲥⲏ.
9	Jesus Christ the mighty ✢ gave grace to the saint ✢ to	ⲓ̅ⲏ̅ⲥ̅ ⲡ̅ⲭ̅ⲥ̅ ⲫⲁ ⲡⲓⲁⲙⲁϩⲓ ✢ ⲁϥϯ ⲛ̀ⲟⲩϩ̀ⲙⲟⲧ ⲉ̀ⲡⲓⲁⲅⲓⲟⲥ ✢ ϩⲓⲛⲁ

perform many wonders ✛ O strong saint, Abba Moses!	ⲛ̀ⲧⲉϥ̀ⲓⲣⲓ ⲛ̀ϩⲁⲛⲙⲏⲓⲛⲓ ✛ ⲡⲓϣⲱⲣⲓ ⲉ̅ⲑ̅ⲩ̅ ⲁⲃⲃⲁ ⲙⲱⲥⲏ.
10 According to the holy saying, ✛ "The righteous shine like the sun ✛ in their Father's Kingdom"[183] ✛ O strong saint, Abba Moses!	ⲕⲁⲧⲁ ⲫⲣⲏϯ ⲉ̀ⲡⲓⲥⲁϫⲓ ⲉ̅ⲑ̅ⲩ̅ ✛ ϫⲉ ⲛⲓⲑ̀ⲙⲏⲓ ⲉⲣⲟⲩⲱⲓⲛⲓ ✛ ϧⲉⲛ ⲑ̀ⲙⲉⲧⲟⲩⲣⲟ ⲛ̀ⲧⲉ ⲡⲟⲩⲓⲱⲧ ✛ ⲡⲓϣⲱⲣⲓ ⲉ̅ⲑ̅ⲩ̅ ⲁⲃⲃⲁ ⲙⲱⲥⲏ.
11 The righteous and the strugglers ✛ the saints and the martyrs ✛ rejoice today with the ascetic ✛ O strong saint, Abba Moses!	ⲗⲟⲓⲡⲟⲛ ⲛⲓⲇⲓⲕⲉⲟⲥ ⲛⲉⲙ ⲛⲓⲁⲑⲗⲓⲧⲏⲥ ✛ ⲛⲓⲑ̀ⲙⲏⲓ ⲛⲉⲙ ⲛⲓⲙⲁⲣⲧⲩⲣⲟⲥ ✛ ⲉⲩⲣⲁϣⲓ ⲙ̀ⲫⲟⲟⲩ ⲛⲉⲙ ⲡⲓⲁⲥⲕⲏⲧⲏⲥ ✛ ⲡⲓϣⲱⲣⲓ ⲉ̅ⲑ̅ⲩ̅ ⲁⲃⲃⲁ ⲙⲱⲥⲏ.
12 Grant me, O Lord, repentance ✛ fill me with many tears ✛ like the struggler ✛ O strong saint, Abba Moses!	ⲙⲟⲓ ⲛⲏⲓ ⲡ̅ⲟ̅ⲥ̅ ⲛ̀ⲧⲁⲓⲙⲟⲓⲧⲁⲛⲓⲁ ✛ ⲙⲁ̀ⲧⲥⲱⲓ ⲛ̀ⲛⲁⲓⲉⲣⲙⲱⲟⲩⲓ ✛ ⲕⲁⲧⲁ ⲡ̀ⲧⲩⲡⲟⲥ ⲙ̀ⲡⲁϣⲓⲣⲓ ✛ ⲡⲓϣⲱⲣⲓ ⲉ̅ⲑ̅ⲩ̅ ⲁⲃⲃⲁ ⲙⲱⲥⲏ.
13 All the thieves in this world ✛ have found an intercessor ✛ a true example ✛ O strong saint, Abba Moses!	ⲛⲓⲥⲓⲛⲓϣⲟⲩⲓ ⲧⲏⲣⲟⲩ ϧⲉⲛ ⲡⲁⲓⲕⲟⲥⲙⲟⲥ ✛ ⲁⲩϫⲓⲙⲓ ⲛⲱⲟⲩ ⲛ̀ⲟⲩⲡ̀ⲣⲟⲥⲧⲁⲧⲏⲥ ✛ ⲟⲩⲧⲩⲡⲟⲥ

---

[183] Matthew 13:43

		ⲋⲟⲗⲝ ⲛ̀ⲁⲗⲓⲑⲉⲛⲟⲥ ✛ ⲡⲓⳉⲱⲣⲓ ⲉ̅ⲑ̅ⲩ̅ ⲁⲃⲃⲁ ⲙⲱⲥⲏ.
14	You exceeded all the monks ✛ you became a guide ✛ in the mountain of Scetis ✛ O strong saint, Abba Moses!	ⲝⲁⲡ̀ϣⲱⲓ ⲛ̀ⲛⲓⲙⲟⲛⲁⲭⲟⲥ ⲧⲏⲣⲟⲩ ✛ ⲁⲕϣⲱⲡⲓ ⲛ̀ⲟⲩⲣⲉϥⲉⲣⲟⲓⲕⲟⲛⲟⲙⲓⲛ ✛ ϧⲉⲛ ⲡ̀ⲧⲱⲟⲩ ⲛ̀ⲧⲉ ϣⲓϩⲏⲧ ✛ ⲡⲓⳉⲱⲣⲓ ⲉ̅ⲑ̅ⲩ̅ ⲁⲃⲃⲁ ⲙⲱⲥⲏ.
15	All pride and radiance ✛ glory and praise ✛ befit the fighter ✛ O strong saint, Abba Moses!	ⲟⲩϣⲟⲩϣⲟⲩ ⲛⲉⲙ ⲟⲩⲙⲉⲧⲗⲁⲙⲡ̀ⲣⲟⲥ ✛ ⲛⲉⲙ ⲟⲩⲱ̀ⲟⲩ ⲛⲉⲙ ⲟⲩϩⲩⲙⲛⲟⲥ ✛ ⲥⲉⲧⲱⲙⲓ ⲉ̀ⲡⲓⲁⲑⲗⲟⲫⲟⲣⲟⲥ ✛ ⲡⲓⳉⲱⲣⲓ ⲉ̅ⲑ̅ⲩ̅ ⲁⲃⲃⲁ ⲙⲱⲥⲏ.
16	You carried a sandbag ✛ on your back with humility ✛ to forgive the sinner ✛ O strong saint, Abba Moses!	ⲡⲁⲗⲓⲛ ⲁⲕⲱⲗⲓ ⲛ̀ⲟⲩϣⲱ ✛ ϩⲓϫⲉⲛ ⲧⲉⲕⲛⲁϩⲡⲓ ϧⲉⲛ ⲟⲩⲑⲉⲃⲓⲟ ✛ ⲉⲑⲣⲟⲩⲭⲱ ⲙ̀ⲡⲓⲣⲉϥⲉⲣⲛⲟⲃⲓ ⲉ̀ⲃⲟⲗ ✛ ⲡⲓⳉⲱⲣⲓ ⲉ̅ⲑ̅ⲩ̅ ⲁⲃⲃⲁ ⲙⲱⲥⲏ.
17	Happily rejoice today ✛ O holy Abba Isidore the priest ✛ for your son ✛ O strong saint, Abba Moses!	ⲣⲁϣⲓ ⲕⲁⲗⲱⲥ ⲱ̀ ⲡⲓⲁⲅⲓⲟⲥ ✛ ⲁⲃⲃⲁ ⲏⲥⲓⲇⲱⲣⲟⲥ ⲡⲓⲡ̀ⲣⲉⲥⲃⲩⲧⲏⲣⲟⲥ ✛ ϧⲉⲛ ⲡⲁⲓⲉ̀ϩⲟⲟⲩ ⲉⲑⲃⲉ ⲡⲉⲕϣⲏⲣⲓ ✛ ⲡⲓⳉⲱⲣⲓ ⲉ̅ⲑ̅ⲩ̅ ⲁⲃⲃⲁ ⲙⲱⲥⲏ.
18	Bless the air of the heaven ✛ the waters and the fruits ✛	ⲥⲙⲟⲩ ⲉⲛⲓⲁⲏⲣ ⲛ̀ⲧⲉ ⲧ̀ⲫⲉ ✛ ⲛⲉⲙ ⲛⲓⲙⲱⲟⲩ ⲛⲉⲙ ⲛⲓⲕⲁⲣⲡⲟⲥ ✛ ⲉⲑⲃⲉ

	for the sake of Your saint ✢ O strong saint, Abba Moses!	ⲡⲉⲕⲥⲱⲧⲡ ⲙ̅ⲫⲛⲉⲑⲟⲩⲁⲃ ✢ ⲡⲓϫⲱⲣⲓ ⲉ̄ⲑ̄ⲩ̄ ⲁⲃⲃⲁ ⲙⲱⲥⲏ.
19	We ask You, O Lover of humanity ✢ receive our struggle ✢ for the sake of our lord and father ✢ O strong saint, Abba Moses!	ⲧⲉⲛⲧⲱⲃϩ ⲙ̅ⲙⲟⲕ ⲱ̇ ⲡⲓⲙⲁⲓⲣⲱⲙⲓ ✢ ϣⲱⲡ ⲉⲣⲟⲕ ⲛ̅ⲛⲉⲛⲁϣⲓⲣⲓ ✢ ⲛⲁϩⲙⲉⲛ ⲉⲑⲃⲉ ⲡⲉⲛⲟ̅ⲥ̅ ⲛ̅ⲓⲱⲧ ✢ ⲡⲓϫⲱⲣⲓ ⲉ̄ⲑ̄ⲩ̄ ⲁⲃⲃⲁ ⲙⲱⲥⲏ.
20	O Son of God, the true physician ✢ grant healing to Your people ✢ for the sake of Your mother and the martyr ✢ O strong saint, Abba Moses!	ⲩⲓⲟⲥ ⲑⲉⲟⲥ ⲡⲓⲥⲏⲓⲛⲓ ⲙ̇ⲙⲏⲓ ✢ ⲙⲟⲓ ⲙ̇ⲡⲓⲧⲁⲗϭⲟ ⲙ̇ⲡⲉⲕⲗⲁⲟⲥ ✢ ⲉⲑⲃⲉ ⲧⲉⲕⲙⲁⲩ ⲛⲉⲙ ⲡⲓⲙⲁⲣⲧⲩⲣⲟⲥ ✢ ⲡⲓϫⲱⲣⲓ ⲉ̄ⲑ̄ⲩ̄ ⲁⲃⲃⲁ ⲙⲱⲥⲏ.
21	O Master God, our helper ✢ keep Your faithful people ✢ and the clergy because of the monk ✢ O strong saint, Abba Moses!	ⲫⲛⲏⲃ ⲫϯ ⲡⲉⲛⲃⲟⲏⲑⲟⲥ ✢ ⲁⲣⲉϩ ⲉ̇ⲡⲉⲕⲗⲁⲟⲥ ⲙ̇ⲡⲓⲥⲧⲟⲥ ✢ ⲛⲉⲙ ⲡⲓⲕ̅ⲗⲏⲣⲟⲥ ⲉⲑⲃⲉ ⲡⲓⲙⲟⲛⲁⲭⲟⲥ ✢ ⲡⲓϫⲱⲣⲓ ⲉ̄ⲑ̄ⲩ̄ ⲁⲃⲃⲁ ⲙⲱⲥⲏ.
22	Hail to you O Virgin! ✢ Hail to you O lover of your children ✢ ask the Lord on	ⲭⲉⲣⲉ ⲛⲉ ⲱ̇ ϯⲡⲁⲣⲑⲉⲛⲟⲥ ✢ ⲭⲉⲣⲉ ⲛⲁⲕ ⲱ̇ ⲡⲓⲙⲁⲓⲛⲉⲕϣⲏⲣⲓ ✢ ⲧⲱⲃϩ ⲙ̇ⲡⲟ̅ⲥ̅ ⲉ̇ϩⲣⲏⲓ ⲉϫⲱⲛ ✢ ⲡⲓϫⲱⲣⲓ ⲉ̄ⲑ̄ⲩ̄ ⲁⲃⲃⲁ ⲙⲱⲥⲏ.

our behalf ✢ O strong saint, Abba Moses!

23 All the souls in all places ✢ praise Christ the King ✢ and hymn His saint ✢ O strong saint, Abba Moses!

ⲯⲩⲭⲏ ⲛⲓⲃⲉⲛ ϧⲉⲛ ⲙⲁⲓ ⲛⲓⲃⲉⲛ ✢ ⲉⲩϩⲱⲥ ⲉ̀ⲡ̀ⲟⲩⲣⲟ ⲡ̅ⲭ̅ⲥ̅ ✢ ⲉⲩⲉⲣⲉⲩⲫⲟⲙⲓⲛ ⲙ̀ⲡⲉϥⲁⲅⲓⲟⲥ ✢ ⲡⲓϫⲱⲣⲓ ⲉ̅ⲑ̅ⲩ̅ ⲁⲃⲃⲁ ⲙⲱⲥⲏ.

24 Blessed is the man ✢ who forsook this life ✢ and all its evil deeds ✢ O strong saint, Abba Moses!

ⲱⲟⲩⲛⲓⲁⲧϥ ⲙ̀ⲡⲓⲣⲱⲙⲓ ✢ ⲫⲏⲉⲧⲁϥⲭⲱ ⲛ̀ⲥⲱϥ ⲙ̀ⲡⲁⲓⲃⲓⲟⲥ ⲫⲁⲓ ✢ ⲛⲉⲙ ⲛⲉϥϩⲃⲏⲟⲩⲓ ⲉⲧϩⲱⲟⲩ ✢ ⲡⲓϫⲱⲣⲓ ⲉ̅ⲑ̅ⲩ̅ ⲁⲃⲃⲁ ⲙⲱⲥⲏ.

25 Our hearts are filled with joy ✢ when we honor ✢ our blessed intercessor ✢ O strong saint, Abba Moses!

ϣⲁϥⲟⲩⲟⲛⲟϥ ⲛ̀ϫⲉ ⲡⲉⲛϩⲏⲧ ✢ ⲉϣⲱⲡ ⲁⲛϣⲁⲛ ⲉⲣⲙⲁⲕⲁⲣⲓⲍⲓⲛ ✢ ⲙ̀ⲡⲉⲛⲙⲁⲕⲁⲣⲓⲟⲥ ⲙ̀ⲡⲣⲟⲥⲧⲁⲧⲏⲥ ✢ ⲡⲓϫⲱⲣⲓ ⲉ̅ⲑ̅ⲩ̅ ⲁⲃⲃⲁ ⲙⲱⲥⲏ.

26 Blessed is your mind! ✢ Blessed is your heart! ✢ O disperser of devils ✢ O strong saint, Abba Moses!

ϥ̀ⲥⲙⲁⲣⲱⲟⲩⲧ ⲛ̀ϫⲉ ⲡⲉⲕⲛⲟⲩⲥ ✢ ϥ̀ⲥⲙⲁⲣⲱⲟⲩⲧ ⲛ̀ϫⲉ ⲡⲉⲕϩⲏⲧ ✢ ⲡⲓⲉⲃⲟⲩϩⲓ ⲛ̀ⲛⲓⲇⲁⲓⲙⲱⲛ ✢ ⲡⲓϫⲱⲣⲓ ⲉ̅ⲑ̅ⲩ̅ ⲁⲃⲃⲁ ⲙⲱⲥⲏ.

27 In Scetis you were transformed ✢ and rested in the Lord ✢ You struggled

ϧⲉⲛ ϣⲓϩⲏⲧ ⲁⲩⲙⲁⲥⲕ ⲛ̀ⲕⲉⲥⲟⲡ ✢ ⲟⲩⲟϩ ⲁⲕⲙ̀ⲧⲟⲛ ϧⲉⲛ ⲡ̅ⲟ̅ⲥ̅ ✢ ⲁⲕⲉⲣϣⲟⲓⲭ ⲟⲩⲟϩ ⲁⲕϭⲣⲟ ✢ ⲡⲓϫⲱⲣⲓ ⲉ̅ⲑ̅ⲩ̅ ⲁⲃⲃⲁ ⲙⲱⲥⲏ.

and were victorious ✛ O strong saint, Abba Moses!

28 At the point of martyrdom ✛ he accepted death to himself ✛ with joy he declared ✛ O strong saint, Abba Moses!

ϩⲁ ⲡⲥⲏⲟⲩ ⲛ̀ⲧⲉ ϯⲙⲉⲧⲙⲁⲣⲧⲩⲣⲓⲁ ✛ ⲁϥϣⲱⲡ ⲉⲣⲟϥ ⲙ̀ⲫⲙⲟⲩ ✛ ϧⲉⲛ ⲟⲩⲣⲁϣⲓ ⲁϥⲟⲩⲱⲛϩ ⲉⲃⲟⲗ ✛ ⲡⲓϫⲱⲣⲓ ⲉ̅ⲑ̅ⲩ̅ ⲁⲃⲃⲁ ⲙⲱⲥⲏ.

29 For with great endurance ✛ he accepted suffering ✛ like a true hero ✛ O strong saint, Abba Moses!

ϫⲉ ϧⲉⲛ ⲟⲩϣ̀ⲫⲏⲣⲓ ⲛ̀ϩⲩⲡⲟⲙⲟⲛⲏ ✛ ⲁϥϣⲱⲡ ⲛ̀ϩⲁⲛⲛⲟϫⲛⲉϫ ✛ ⲕⲁⲧⲁ ⲫⲣⲏϯ ⲛ̀ⲟⲩⲃⲁⲥⲁⲛⲟⲥ ✛ ⲡⲓϫⲱⲣⲓ ⲉ̅ⲑ̅ⲩ̅ ⲁⲃⲃⲁ ⲙⲱⲥⲏ.

30 Be bright and full of light ✛ O mountain of Scetis ✛ on the feast of your intercessor ✛ O strong saint, Abba Moses!

Ϭⲓⲟⲩⲱⲓⲛⲓ ϭⲓⲟⲩⲱⲓⲛⲓ ✛ ⲱ̀ ⲡⲓⲧⲱⲟⲩ ⲛ̀ϣⲓϩⲧ ✛ ϧⲉⲛ ⲡ̀ϣⲁⲓ ⲙ̀ⲡⲉⲕⲡ̀ⲣⲟⲥⲧⲁⲧⲏⲥ ✛ ⲡⲓϫⲱⲣⲓ ⲉ̅ⲑ̅ⲩ̅ ⲁⲃⲃⲁ ⲙⲱⲥⲏ.

31 Grant us Your true peace ✛ for the sake of Your mother the virgin ✛ and the Spirit-bearer ✛ O strong saint, Abba Moses!

ϯⲛⲁⲛ ⲛ̀ⲧⲉⲕϩⲓⲣⲏⲛⲏ ⲙ̀ⲙⲏⲓ ✛ ⲉⲑⲃⲉ ⲧⲉⲕⲙⲁⲩ ⲙ̀ⲡⲁⲣⲑⲉⲛⲟⲥ ✛ ⲛⲉⲙ ⲡⲓⲡ̀ⲛⲉⲩⲙⲁⲧⲟⲫⲟⲣⲟⲥ ✛ ⲡⲓϫⲱⲣⲓ ⲉ̅ⲑ̅ⲩ̅ ⲁⲃⲃⲁ ⲙⲱⲥⲏ.

ANTIPHONARY[184]

1	We worship the good Father, and His Son Jesus Christ, and the Spirit of comfort, the Holy Trinity, of one essence.	ⲧⲉⲛⲟⲩⲱϣⲧ ⲙ̀ⲫⲓⲱⲧ ⲛ̀ⲁⲅⲁⲑⲟⲥ ✤ ⲛⲉⲙ ⲡⲉϥϣⲏⲣⲓ I̅H̅C̅ P̅X̅C̅ ✤ ⲛⲉⲙ ⲡⲓⲡⲛⲉⲩⲙⲁ ⲙ̀ⲡⲁⲣⲁⲕⲗⲏⲧⲟⲛ ✤ †ⲧⲣⲓⲁⲥ ⲉ̅ⲑ̅ⲩ̅ ⲛ̀ⲟⲙⲟⲟⲩⲥⲓⲟⲥ.
2	Hail to you, O Virgin! The righteous and true queen. Hail to the pride of our race, who bore for us Emmanuel.	ⲭⲉⲣⲉ ⲛⲉ ⲱ̀ †ⲡⲁⲣⲑⲉⲛⲟⲥ ✤ †ⲟⲩⲣⲱ ⲙ̀ⲙⲏⲓ ⲛ̀ⲁⲗⲏⲑⲓⲛⲓ ✤ ⲭⲉⲣⲉ ⲡ̀ϣⲟⲩϣⲟⲩ ⲛ̀ⲧⲉ ⲡⲉⲛⲅⲉⲛⲟⲥ ✤ ⲁ̀ⲣⲉϫ̀ⲫⲟ ⲛⲁⲛ ⲛ̀ⲉⲙⲙⲁⲛⲟⲩⲏⲗ.

In the Adam Tune

3	Come to us today ✤ O Abba Isidore ✤ the priest ✤ of our church	ⲁⲙⲟⲩ ϣⲁⲣⲟⲛ ⲙ̀ⲫⲟⲟⲩ ✤ ⲱ̀ ⲁⲃⲃⲁ ⲓⲥⲓⲇⲱⲣⲟⲥ ✤ ⲡⲓⲡ̀ⲣⲉⲥⲃⲩⲧⲉⲣⲟⲥ ✤ ⲛ̀ⲧⲉ ⲧⲉⲛⲉⲕⲕⲗⲏⲥⲓⲁ.

---

[184] De Lacy O'Leary, *The Difnar (Antiphonarium) of the Coptic Church, Vol. 3: Bashons, Baounah, Abib, Mesre and the intercalary days or Nasi* (London, 1930), 22. There are Coptic texts missing in O'Leary's edition that Gawdat Gabra found in the manuscripts of St. Antony's Monastery. He provides a German translation of the text: "Bemerkungen zu Moses dem Schwartzen," in ΘΕΜΕΛΙΑ: Spätantike und koptologische Studien Peter Grossmann zum 65, Geburstag, ed. M. Krause, S. Schaten, (Wiesbaden, 1998): 121–124.

4	and detail to us ✣ the elect life of ✣ Abba Moses ✣ beginning with his youth	ⲛⲧⲉⲕϩⲓⲥⲧⲟⲣⲓⲛ ⲛⲁⲛ ✣ ⲙ̄ⲡⲃⲓⲟⲥ ⲉⲧⲥⲱⲧⲡ ✣ ⲛ̄ⲧⲉ ⲁⲃⲃⲁ ⲙⲱⲥⲏ ✣ ⲓⲥϫⲉⲛ ⲧⲉϥⲙⲉⲧⲕⲟⲩϫⲓ.
5	For you are he who brought him ✣ to Abba Macarius ✣ the illuminator ✣ of our assembly	ϫⲉ ⲛ̄ⲑⲟⲕ ⲡⲉ ⲁⲕⲉⲛϥ ✣ ϣⲁ ⲁⲃⲃⲁ ⲙⲁⲕⲁⲣⲓ ✣ ⲡⲓⲣⲉϥⲉⲣⲟⲩⲱⲓⲛⲓ ✣ ⲛ̄ⲧⲉ ⲧⲉⲛⲥⲩⲛⲟⲩⲇⲓⲁ.
6	He became ✣ a spiritual son ✣ to both of you ✣ and revealed to you his secrets	ⲁϥϣⲱⲡⲓ ⲛⲱⲧⲉⲛ ⲛ̄ⲟⲩϣⲏⲣⲓ ✣ ⲙ̄ⲡ̄ⲛⲉⲩⲙⲁⲧⲓⲕⲟⲥ ✣ ⲁϥⲟⲩⲱⲛϩ ⲉⲣⲱⲧⲉⲛ ✣ ⲛ̄ⲛⲏⲉⲧϩⲏⲡ ⲛ̄ⲧⲁϥ.

7 By the command of God, Abba Moses came into the holy mountain of Abba Macarius. When Abba Isidore met him, he became fearful by his appearance. For he was very tall like a giant, having a broad body and being fiercely unbeatable. He spoke with him to test him and see if he would turn back to his old ways. He said, "We are oppressed by the devils. You cannot be with us. We suffer because of the scarcity and can barely meet our needs. We gain no pleasure anywhere. Go, my son, to the land of Egypt, there you may live as you wish." Abba Moses being pleased with Abba Macarius and Abba Isidore, said, "For the sake of God the Most High, accept me to you, my saintly fathers and true physicians."

7 ϧⲉⲛ ⲟⲩⲥⲱⲛ ⲛ̀ⲧⲉ ⲫϯ ⲁϥⲓ̀ ⲛ̀ϫⲉ ⲁⲃⲃⲁ ⲙⲟⲩⲥⲏ ϣⲁ ⲡⲓⲧⲱⲟⲩ ⲉ̅ⲑ̅ⲩ̅ ✢ ⲛ̀ⲧⲉ ⲁⲃⲃⲁ ⲙⲁⲕⲁⲣⲓ ⲁϥϯⲙⲁϯ ⲉ̀ⲣⲟϥ ⲛ̀ϫⲉ ⲁⲃⲃⲁ ⲓ̀ⲥⲓⲇⲱⲣⲟⲥ ⲁϥϣⲱⲡⲓ ϧⲉⲛ ⲟⲩϩⲟϯ ϩⲓⲧⲉⲛ ⲡⲉϥϫⲓⲛ ⲛⲁⲩ ϫⲉ ⲛⲁϥϭⲟⲥⲓ ⲉ̀ⲙⲁϣⲱ ⲙ̀ⲫⲣⲏϯ ⲛ̀ⲟⲩⲁⲫⲱϣ ⲉϥⲟⲩⲉⲥⲑⲱⲛ ϧⲉⲛ ⲡⲉϥⲥⲱⲙⲁ ⲉϥⲙⲉϩ ⲛ̀ϫⲟⲙ ⲛ̀ⲛⲟⲙϯ ⲁϥⲥⲁϫⲓ ⲛⲉⲙⲁϥ ⲉϥⲇⲟⲕⲓⲙⲏ ⲙ̀ⲙⲟϥ ϫⲉ ⲁ̀ⲣⲏⲟⲩ ϥ̀ⲛⲁⲧⲁⲥⲑⲟϥ ⲉ̀ⲫⲁϩⲟⲩ ⲛ̀ⲕⲉⲥⲟⲡ ⲡⲉϫⲁϥ ϫⲉ ⲧⲉⲛϩⲉⲭⲣⲱϧ ⲛ̀ⲧⲟⲧⲟⲩ ⲛ̀ⲛⲓⲇⲉⲙⲱⲛ ⲙ̀ⲙⲟⲛ ϣ̀ϫⲟⲙ ⲙ̀ⲙⲟⲕ ⲉ̀ϣⲱⲡⲓ ϩⲁ ⲧⲱⲧⲉⲛ ⲧⲉⲛϩⲉⲭⲣⲱϧ ⲉⲑⲃⲉ ⲡϣⲱⲧ ⲛ̀ⲧⲉⲛ ⲉⲣⲭ̀ⲣⲓⲁ̀ ⲙ̀ⲙⲟⲛ ⲟⲩⲛⲟϥ ϣⲟⲡ ⲛⲁⲛ ⲉ̀ⲃⲟⲗ ϧⲉⲛ ϩ̀ⲗⲓ ⲛ̀ⲥⲁ ⲙⲁϣⲉⲛⲁⲕ ⲡⲁϣⲏⲣⲓ ⲉⲡ̀ⲕⲁϩⲓ ⲛ̀ⲭⲏⲙⲓ ⲭ̀ⲛⲁϣⲱⲛϧ ⲙ̀ⲙⲁⲩ ⲕⲁⲧⲁ ⲡⲉⲧⲉϩⲛⲁⲕ ⲛⲁϥϯϩⲟ ⲉ̀ⲣⲱⲟⲩ ⲡⲉ ⲛ̀ϫⲉ ⲁⲃⲃⲁ ⲙⲟⲩⲥⲏ ⲉ̀ⲧⲉ ⲁⲃⲃⲁ ⲙⲁⲕⲁⲣⲓ ⲛⲉⲙ ⲁⲡⲁ ⲓ̀ⲥⲓⲇⲱⲣⲟⲥ ϫⲉ ⲉⲑⲃⲉ ⲫϯ ⲉⲧϭⲟⲥⲓ ⲱ̀ ⲛⲁⲓⲟϯ ⲉ̅ⲑ̅ⲩ̅ ⲛ̀ⲧⲉⲧⲉⲛϣⲟⲡⲧ ⲉ̀ⲣⲱⲧⲉⲛ ϩⲁ ⲛⲓϣⲏⲣⲓ ⲙ̀ⲙⲏⲓ

Before the icon of Abba Moses

8 "Do not cast me out ✢ from under the refuge of your prayers ✢ O truly wise men ✢ and saviors of souls.	ⲙ̀ⲡⲉⲣϩⲓⲧ ⲥⲁⲃⲟⲗ ✢ ϩⲁ ⲧ̀ⲥⲕⲉⲡⲓ ⲛ̀ⲛⲉⲧⲉⲛϣ̀ⲗⲏⲗ ✢ ⲱ̀ ⲛⲓⲥⲟⲫⲟⲥ ⲙ̀ⲙⲏⲓ ✢ ⲉ̀ⲑⲛⲟϩⲉⲙ ⲛ̀ⲛⲓⲯⲩⲭⲏ.
9 For I have been persecuted ✢ by Satan ✢ he made me poor ✢ by his wickedness.	ϫⲉ ⲟⲩⲏⲓ ⲁϥϯϩⲉⲙⲕⲟⲓ ✢ ⲛ̀ϫⲉ ⲡⲥⲁⲧⲁⲛⲁⲥ ✢ ⲁϥⲓ̀ⲣⲓ ⲙ̀ⲙⲟⲓ ⲛ̀ϩⲏⲕⲓ ✢ ⲛ̀ϧ̀ⲣⲏⲓ ϧⲉⲛ ⲧⲉϥⲕⲁⲕⲓⲁ.
10 For the sake of God ✢ give me a saving remedy ✢ that I may be delivered ✢ from this torment."	ⲉⲑⲃⲉ ⲫϯ ⲙⲟⲓ ⲛⲏⲓ ✢ ⲛ̀ⲟⲩⲫⲁϧⲣⲓ ⲛ̀ⲟⲩϫⲁⲓ ✢ ϩⲓⲛⲁ ⲛ̀ⲧⲁⲛⲟϩⲉⲙ ⲛ̀ⲧⲟⲧϥ ✢ ⲉ̀ⲃⲟⲗ ϧⲉⲛ ⲡⲁⲓⲃⲁⲥⲁⲛⲟⲥ.

11	"In this case ✛ the Lord is pleased ✛ for you to dwell with us ✛ O Moses the Black.	ⲓⲥϫⲉ ⲟⲛ ⲡⲁⲓⲣⲏϯ ✛ ⲁϥϯⲙⲁϯ ⲛ̀ϫⲉ ⲡϭⲟⲓⲥ ✛ ⲉⲑⲣⲉⲕϣⲱⲡⲓ ⲛⲉⲙⲁⲕ ✛ ⲱ̀ ⲙⲱⲩⲥⲏⲥ ⲡⲓⲭⲁⲙⲏ.
12	Leave behind your old habits ✛ that does not ✛ offer salvation ✛ and invigorate yourself	ⲓⲧⲁ ⲕⲱ ⲛ̀ⲥⲱⲕ ⲛ̀ⲛⲉⲕⲥⲩⲛⲏⲑⲓⲁ ✛ ⲉⲧⲁⲕⲉⲣϩⲱⲃ ⲛ̀ϧⲏⲧⲟⲩ ✛ ϧⲉⲛ ⲟⲩⲙⲉⲧⲁⲧⲟⲩϫⲁⲓ ✛ ⲁⲣⲓ ⲁϣⲓⲣⲓ ⲉⲣⲟⲕ
13	With devotion ✛ and virtue ✛ which lead you ✛ to our way of life.	ϧⲉⲛ ⲛⲓⲡⲟⲗⲏⲧⲩⲓⲁ ✛ ⲛⲉⲙ ⲛⲓⲁ̀ⲣⲉⲧⲏ ✛ ⲉⲧϭⲓ ⲉ̀ϧⲟⲩⲛ ✛ ⲉⲡⲉⲛⲃⲓⲟⲥ.

14 Take fasting unto yourself, for with it you overcome everything; and meekness, so that you might overcome anger. Love purity and hate desire. Abhor the will to covet and you will triumph everything." By the good will of God the Word, they instructed him with the words of God. Our saintly fathers baptized him and ministered to him the body and blood of Christ and made him a man deserving of Christ. In him, the words of David were fulfilled, "Purge me with your hyssop and I will be made clean; wash me, and I will become whiter than snow!"[185]

---

[185] Ps. 51:7

14 ⲕⲱ ⲛⲁⲕ ⲛ̀ⲧⲛⲏⲥⲧⲓⲁ ⲕⲛⲁϭⲣⲟ ⲉⲡϫⲱⲛⲧ ⲙⲉⲛⲣⲉ ⲡⲓⲧⲟⲩⲃⲟ ⲙⲉⲥⲧⲉ ϯϩⲩⲗⲏ ⲕⲛⲁϭⲣⲟ ⲉϩⲱⲃ ⲛⲓⲃⲉⲛ ⲕⲁⲧⲁ ⲟⲩϯⲙⲁϯ ⲛ̀ⲧⲉ ⲫϯ ⲡⲓⲗⲟⲅⲟⲥ ⲁⲩⲉⲣⲕⲁⲑⲏⲭⲓⲛ ⲙ̀ⲙⲟϥ ϧⲉⲛ ⲡⲓⲥⲁϫⲓ ⲛ̀ⲧⲉ ⲫϯ ⲟⲩⲟϩ ⲁⲩⲧⲱⲙⲥ ⲛⲁϥ ⲛ̀ϫⲉ ⲛⲉⲛⲓⲟϯ ⲉ̅ⲑ̅ⲩ̅ ⲁⲩϯ ⲛⲁϥ ⲙ̀ⲡⲓⲥⲱⲙⲁ ⲛⲉⲙ ⲡⲓⲥⲛⲟϥ ⲙ̀ⲡⲭ̅ⲥ̅ ⲁϥϫⲱⲕ ⲉⲃⲟⲗ ⲉϫⲱϥ ⲛ̀ϫⲉ ⲡⲥⲁϫⲓ ⲛ̀ⲇⲁⲩⲓⲇ ⲉⲕⲉⲛⲟⲩϧ ⲉϫⲱⲓ ⲙ̀ⲡⲉⲕϣⲉ ⲛ̀ϩⲩⲥⲱⲡⲟⲛ ⲉⲕⲉⲣⲁϧⲧ ⲉⲓⲉⲟⲩⲁϣ ⲉϩⲟⲧⲉ ⲟⲩⲭⲓⲱⲛ

In the Watos Tune

15 Come, look and marvel ✛ my fathers the monks ✛ for a thief ✛ has snatched Paradise.

ⲁⲙⲱⲓⲛⲓ ⲁ̀ⲛⲁⲩ ⲁ̀ⲣⲓϣ̀ⲫⲏⲣⲓ ✛ ⲱ̀ ⲛⲁⲓⲟϯ ⲙ̀ⲙⲟⲛⲁⲭⲟⲥ ✛ ⲟⲩⲥⲟⲛ ⲛ̀ⲣⲉϥϭⲱⲧⲉⲃ ✛ ⲁϥⲱⲗⲉⲙ ⲉ̀ⲡⲓⲡⲁⲣⲁⲇⲓⲥⲟⲥ.

16 In him was fulfilled ✛ the words of our Saviour ✛ in the Holy Gospel ✛ as He thus said,

ⲁϥϫⲱⲕ ⲉⲃⲟⲗ ⲉ̀ϩⲣⲏⲓ ⲉ̀ϫⲱϥ ✛ ⲛ̀ϫⲉ ⲡⲓⲥⲁϫⲓ ⲙ̀ⲡⲉⲛⲥⲱⲧⲏⲣ ✛ ϧⲉⲛ ⲡⲓⲉⲩⲁⲅⲅⲉⲗⲓⲟⲛ ⲉⲑⲟⲩⲁⲃ ✛ ⲙ̀ⲡⲁⲓⲣⲏϯ ⲉϥϫⲱ ⲙ̀ⲙⲟⲥ.

17 "The violent have entered ✛ the Kingdom of Heaven ✛ by the power ✛ of the Holy Spirit." [186]

ϫⲉ ϩⲁⲛⲟⲩⲟⲛ ⲛ̀ϭⲓⲛ̀ϫⲟⲛⲥ ✛ ⲉⲩϩⲱⲗ ⲛ̀ϯⲙⲉⲧⲟⲩⲣⲟ ✛ ⲛ̀ⲧⲉ ⲛⲓⲫⲏⲟⲩⲓ ϧⲉⲛ ϯϫⲟⲙ ✛ ⲛ̀ⲧⲉ ⲡⲓⲡ̅ⲛ̅ⲁ̅ ⲉⲑⲟⲩⲁⲃ.

18 One of them ✛ is Abba Moses the Black ✛ For he

ⲉⲧⲉ ⲉⲃⲟⲗ ⲛ̀ϧⲁⲉ ⲧⲟⲩⲡⲉ ✛ ⲁⲃⲃⲁ ⲙⲱⲥⲏ ⲡⲓⲭⲁⲙⲏ ✛ ϫⲉ ⲁϥϣⲱⲡⲓ

---

[186] Matt. 11:12

was a murderer + a glutton and a drunk.	ⲛ̀ⲟⲩⲣⲉϥϧⲱⲧⲉⲃ + ⲛ̀ⲟⲩⲣⲉϥⲟⲩⲱⲙ ⲟⲩⲟϩ ⲛ̀ⲟⲩⲣⲉϥⲑⲓϧⲓ.

19 Jesus Christ chose him for the priesthood. He became a father to many by the Lord's will. He performed many miracles and wonders through the Holy Spirit and completed his journey in a healthy old age, departing with the company of elders to our father Abba Macarius who told them, "One of you will become a martyr." Our father, Abba Moses said, "May this person be me, my father? For he who kills by the sword, dies by the sword."

The Berbers came and killed him along with seven others of the brethren, for they had not wanted to flee until they received the incorruptible crown. But one of them fled and hid. He looked and saw the angel of the Lord carrying the crown in his hands. He quickly came out before the Berbers, and he too received the crown of life from the hand of the angel.

My fathers, look and marvel! The thief, the degenerate, the robber, who never knew God, was baptized, and became a monk and a priest, clothed by the sign of the glorious cross, and attained the crown of martyrdom.

19 Ⲓⲏⲥ Ⲡⲭⲥ ⲁϥⲥⲱⲧⲡ ⲙ̀ⲙⲟϥ ⲛ̀ϯⲙⲉⲧⲡⲣⲉⲥⲃⲩⲧⲉⲣⲟⲥ ⲁϥϣⲱⲡⲓ ⲛ̀ⲟⲩⲓⲱⲧ ⲛ̀ϩⲁⲛⲙⲏϣ ⲕⲁⲧⲁ ⲫⲟⲩⲁϩⲥⲁϩⲛⲓ ⲛ̀ⲧⲉ Ⲡ̅ⲟ̅ⲥ̅ ϩⲁⲛⲙⲏϣ ⲙ̀ⲙⲏⲓⲛⲓ ⲛⲉⲙ ϩⲁⲛϣ̀ⲫⲏⲣⲓ ⲁϥⲁⲓⲧⲟⲩ ϧⲉⲛ ⲡⲓⲡ̅ⲛ̅ⲁ̅ ⲉ̅ⲑ̅ ⲁϥϫⲏⲕ ⲡⲉϥⲇⲣⲟⲙⲟⲥ ⲉⲃⲟⲗ ϧⲉⲛ ⲟⲩⲙⲉⲧϧⲉⲗⲗⲟ ⲉⲛⲁⲛⲉⲥ ⲁϥϣⲉ ⲛⲁϥ ⲛⲉⲙ ⲛⲓϩⲉⲗⲗⲟⲓ ϣⲁ ⲡⲉⲛⲓⲱⲧ ⲁⲃⲃⲁ ⲙⲁⲕⲁⲣⲓ ⲡⲉϫⲁϥ ϫⲉ ⲟⲩⲁⲓ ⲙ̀ⲙⲱⲧⲉⲛ ⲉϥⲉϣⲱⲡⲓ ⲛⲟⲩⲙⲁⲣⲧⲩⲣⲟⲥ ⲡⲉϫⲉ ⲡⲉⲛⲓⲱⲧ ⲁⲃⲃⲁ ⲙⲟⲩⲥⲏ ϫⲉ ϩⲁⲣⲁ ⲁⲛⲟⲕ ⲡⲉ ⲡⲁⲓⲱⲧ ϫⲉ ⲫⲏ ⲉⲑⲛⲁϧⲱⲧⲉⲃ ϧⲉⲛ ⲧⲥⲏϥⲓ ⲥⲉⲛⲁ ϩⲟⲑⲃⲉϥ ϧⲉⲛ ⲧⲥⲏϥⲓ ⲁⲩⲓ ⲛ̀ϫⲉ ⲛⲓⲃⲁⲣⲃⲁⲣⲟⲥ ⲁⲩϧⲟⲑⲃⲉϥ ⲛⲉⲙ Ⲍ̄ ⲛⲥⲟⲛ ϫⲉ ⲙ̀ⲡⲟⲩⲟⲩⲱϣ ⲉⲫⲱⲧ ⲉⲃⲟⲗ ϣⲁⲧⲟⲩϭⲓ ⲙ̀ⲡⲓⲭⲗⲟⲙ ⲛ̀ⲁⲑⲗⲱⲙ ⲁϥⲫⲱⲧ ⲛ̀ϫⲉ ⲟⲩⲁⲓ ⲛ̀ϩⲏⲧⲟⲩ ⲁϥⲉⲣⲁⲑⲟⲩⲱⲛϩ ⲉⲣⲱⲟⲩ ⲁϥⲛⲁⲩ ⲉⲡⲓⲁⲅⲅⲉⲗⲟⲥ ⲛ̀ⲧⲉ ⲡ̅ⲟ̅ⲥ̅ ⲟⲩⲟϩ ⲡⲓⲭⲗⲟⲙ ⲭⲏ ϧⲉⲛ ⲛⲉϥϫⲓϫ ⲥⲁⲧⲟⲧϥ ⲁϥⲓ ⲉⲃⲟⲗ ⲛ̀ⲭⲱⲗⲉⲙ ⲙ̀ⲡⲉⲙⲑⲟ ⲛ̀ⲛⲓⲃⲁⲣⲃⲁⲣⲟⲥ ⲁϥϭⲓ ⲙ̀ⲡⲓⲭⲗⲟⲙ ⲛ̀ⲧⲉ ⲡⲱⲛϩ ϧⲉⲛ ⲧ̀ϫⲓϫ ⲙ̀ⲡⲓⲁⲅⲅⲉⲗⲟⲥ ⲁⲛⲁⲩ ⲛⲁⲓⲟϯ ⲁⲣⲓ ⲫ̀ⲫⲏⲣⲓ ϫⲉ ⲡⲓⲥⲟⲛⲓ ⲛ̀ⲣⲉϥϧⲱⲧⲉⲃ ⲛ̀ⲣⲉϥⲉⲣⲛⲱⲓⲕ ⲛ̀ⲣⲉϥϣⲱⲗⲉⲙ ⲙ̀ⲡⲉϥⲥⲟⲩⲉⲛ ⲫϯ ⲉⲡⲧⲏⲣϥ ⲁϥϭⲓⲱⲙⲥ ⲁϥⲉⲣⲙⲟⲛⲁⲭⲟⲥ ⲁϥϣⲉⲡ ϯⲙⲉⲧⲡⲣⲉⲥⲃⲩⲧⲉⲣⲟⲥ ⲁϥⲉⲣⲫⲟⲣⲓⲛ ⲙ̀ⲡⲓⲥⲧⲁⲩⲣⲟⲥ ⲛⲉⲙ ⲡⲓⲭⲗⲟⲙ ⲛ̀ⲧⲉ ⲛⲓⲙⲁⲣⲧⲩⲣⲟⲥ.

MELODY

1. In the church of the firstborn ✣ in the pure assembly
   ✣ living in all piety ✣ ⲡⲓϫⲱⲣⲓ ⲁⲃⲃⲁ ⲙⲱⲥⲏ
2. He was an idolator ✣ a fierce highway robber
   ✣ he inquired about the Judge ✣ ⲡⲓϫⲱⲣⲓ ⲁⲃⲃⲁ ⲙⲱⲥⲏ
3. Moses was a barbarian ✣ his life was full of sin
   ✣ he yearned to be purified ✣ ⲡⲓϫⲱⲣⲓ ⲁⲃⲃⲁ ⲙⲱⲥⲏ
4. A thief, murderer, and adulterer ✣ lover of this passing world
   ✣ the precious blood washed him ✣ ⲡⲓϫⲱⲣⲓ ⲁⲃⲃⲁ ⲙⲱⲥⲏ
5. Moses the thirsty heard ✣ of our fathers the monks
   ✣ the dwellers of Scetis ✣ ⲡⲓϫⲱⲣⲓ ⲁⲃⲃⲁ ⲙⲱⲥⲏ
6. He asked, "Is there a God ✣ great and awesome?
   ✣ My heart yearns for Him" ✣ ⲡⲓϫⲱⲣⲓ ⲁⲃⲃⲁ ⲙⲱⲥⲏ
7. Abba Isidore answered, ✣ "He took the form of man
   ✣ all heads bow to Him" ✣ ⲡⲓϫⲱⲣⲓ ⲁⲃⲃⲁ ⲙⲱⲥⲏ
8. "Our God is merciful ✣ He accepts the repentant
   ✣ through love, He accepted shame" ✣ ⲡⲓϫⲱⲣⲓ ⲁⲃⲃⲁ ⲙⲱⲥⲏ
9. "Give your life to Him ✣ abandon your past through Him
   ✣ by grace, repent in His hands" ✣ ⲡⲓϫⲱⲣⲓ ⲁⲃⲃⲁ ⲙⲱⲥⲏ

10. Moses stood and said, ✟ "Receive me like the lost son
    ✟ help me to repent now!" ✟ ⲡⲓϫⲱⲣⲓ ⲁⲃⲃⲁ ⲙⲱⲥⲏ
11. With tears and joy ✟ with groaning and delight
    ✟ he repented of his past ✟ ⲡⲓϫⲱⲣⲓ ⲁⲃⲃⲁ ⲙⲱⲥⲏ
12. He approached Christ with love ✟ heartbroken and wounded
    ✟ he hoped to gain rest ✟ ⲡⲓϫⲱⲣⲓ ⲁⲃⲃⲁ ⲙⲱⲥⲏ
13. He offered true repentance ✟ openly without turning back
    ✟ revealing all his sins ✟ ⲡⲓϫⲱⲣⲓ ⲁⲃⲃⲁ ⲙⲱⲥⲏ
14. Lo, an angel of light ✟ wiped away his black sins
    ✟ the tablet became pure white ✟ ⲡⲓϫⲱⲣⲓ ⲁⲃⲃⲁ ⲙⲱⲥⲏ
15. Abba Macarius witnessed ✟ that his Lord redeemed him
    ✟ a new life was granted him ✟ ⲡⲓϫⲱⲣⲓ ⲁⲃⲃⲁ ⲙⲱⲥⲏ
16. He received the first mystery ✟ by water, Spirit and fire
    ✟ removing all impurities ✟ ⲡⲓϫⲱⲣⲓ ⲁⲃⲃⲁ ⲙⲱⲥⲏ
17. Repentance is amazing ✟ a kindling fire in the heart
    ✟ the stranger becomes a friend ✟ ⲡⲓϫⲱⲣⲓ ⲁⲃⲃⲁ ⲙⲱⲥⲏ
18. The murderer became righteous ✟ the sinner, an elect vessel
    ✟ the robber among the elect ✟ ⲡⲓϫⲱⲣⲓ ⲁⲃⲃⲁ ⲙⲱⲥⲏ
19. Repentance is powerful ✟ making the adulterous a virgin
    ✟ and the doubtful accepted ✟ ⲡⲓϫⲱⲣⲓ ⲁⲃⲃⲁ ⲙⲱⲥⲏ

20. A servant of desires and shame ✣ received dignity through grace
    ✣ becoming the strongest of the free ✣ ⲡⲓⲭⲱⲣⲓ ⲁⲃⲃⲁ ⲙⲱⲥⲏ
21. The spirit guided the tyrant ✣ from darkness to light
    ✣ producing fruits for His beloved ✣ ⲡⲓⲭⲱⲣⲓ ⲁⲃⲃⲁ ⲙⲱⲥⲏ
22. He longed for monastic life ✣ and vowed to walk upright
    ✣ God revealed to him the path ✣ ⲡⲓⲭⲱⲣⲓ ⲁⲃⲃⲁ ⲙⲱⲥⲏ
23. His asceticism surpassed others ✣ he served the other monks
    ✣ with humility and vigils ✣ ⲡⲓⲭⲱⲣⲓ ⲁⲃⲃⲁ ⲙⲱⲥⲏ
24. With diligence, he tired himself ✣ walking thousands of miles
    ✣ to fill their water jars ✣ ⲡⲓⲭⲱⲣⲓ ⲁⲃⲃⲁ ⲙⲱⲥⲏ
25. He progressed in the way ✣ in firmness and diligence
    ✣ and growth in righteousness ✣ ⲡⲓⲭⲱⲣⲓ ⲁⲃⲃⲁ ⲙⲱⲥⲏ
26. In virtues and prayers ✣ in fasting and temperance
    ✣ with fear and prostrations ✣ ⲡⲓⲭⲱⲣⲓ ⲁⲃⲃⲁ ⲙⲱⲥⲏ
27. A devout and true ascetic ✣ a strong and firm faith
    ✣ terrifying the demons ✣ ⲡⲓⲭⲱⲣⲓ ⲁⲃⲃⲁ ⲙⲱⲥⲏ
28. He was loved by the brethren ✣ they chose him for priesthood
    ✣ they made known their yearning for ✣ ⲡⲓⲭⲱⲣⲓ ⲁⲃⲃⲁ ⲙⲱⲥⲏ
29. When they tested him ✣ the priests roused and expelled him
    ✣ he obeyed their command ✣ ⲡⲓⲭⲱⲣⲓ ⲁⲃⲃⲁ ⲙⲱⲥⲏ

30. He said, "I am not worthy ✦ they banished you, O black one
    ✦ O you dark skinned man!" ✦ ⲡⲓϫⲱⲣⲓ ⲁⲃⲃⲁ ⲙⲱⲥⲏ

31. The patriarch heard this ✦ he learned of his righteous deeds
    ✦ his humble and perfect soul ✦ ⲡⲓϫⲱⲣⲓ ⲁⲃⲃⲁ ⲙⲱⲥⲏ

32. He ordained him by God's word ✦ a voice said 'ⲁⳌⲓⲟⲥ'
    ✦ all the souls heard this ✦ ⲡⲓϫⲱⲣⲓ ⲁⲃⲃⲁ ⲙⲱⲥⲏ

33. Blessed are you, O Moses! ✦ you received your King's praises
    ✦ the Lord of the vine guarded you ✦ ⲡⲓϫⲱⲣⲓ ⲁⲃⲃⲁ ⲙⲱⲥⲏ

34. Once they invited you ✦ for the case of a sinful monk
    ✦ in the assembly to judge him ✦ ⲡⲓϫⲱⲣⲓ ⲁⲃⲃⲁ ⲙⲱⲥⲏ

35. Saint Moses came to them ✦ a sandbag on his back
    ✦ he entered in dismay ✦ ⲡⲓϫⲱⲣⲓ ⲁⲃⲃⲁ ⲙⲱⲥⲏ

36. They asked him about the bag ✦ what was it that he had
    ✦ he said it was his sins ✦ ⲡⲓϫⲱⲣⲓ ⲁⲃⲃⲁ ⲙⲱⲥⲏ

37. A famed helpful lesson ✦ the monks received in joy
    ✦ they forgave the poor sinner ✦ ⲡⲓϫⲱⲣⲓ ⲁⲃⲃⲁ ⲙⲱⲥⲏ

38. We wish to live your life ✦ we wish to be like you
    ✦ remember us in your prayers ✦ ⲡⲓϫⲱⲣⲓ ⲁⲃⲃⲁ ⲙⲱⲥⲏ

39. Before the exalted throne ✦ before God the great
    ✦ remember us our beloved father ✦ ⲡⲓϫⲱⲣⲓ ⲁⲃⲃⲁ ⲙⲱⲥⲏ

40. Pope Abba [ⲛⲓⲙ] the great ✚ may God grant him long life
    ✚ to preach the gospel ✚ ⲡⲓϪⲱⲣⲓ ⲁⲃⲃⲁ ⲙⲱⲥⲏ
41. Abba [ⲛⲓⲙ] our bishop ✚ keep him and us, O lord
    ✚ by his prayers, protect us ✚ ⲡⲓϪⲱⲣⲓ ⲁⲃⲃⲁ ⲙⲱⲥⲏ
42. The bishops and clergy ✚ guard them, O Holy One
    ✚ with the ranks of ⲛⲓⲁⲅⲅⲉⲗⲟⲥ ✚ ⲡⲓϪⲱⲣⲓ ⲁⲃⲃⲁ ⲙⲱⲥⲏ
43. The deacons and monks ✚ the servants in every place
    ✚ Lord, fill them all with faith ✚ ⲡⲓϪⲱⲣⲓ ⲁⲃⲃⲁ ⲙⲱⲥⲏ
44. Blessed are you, O Moses! ✚ you received your King's praises
    ✚ the Lord of the vine guarded you ✚ ⲡⲓϪⲱⲣⲓ ⲁⲃⲃⲁ ⲙⲱⲥⲏ
45. The mention of your name ✚ is on the believers' lips
    ✚ they all say "O God of Abba Moses ✚ help all of us!"

ANOTHER MELODY

1. He who recalls his sins ✢ and turns his way to God
   ✢ the heavens rejoice for him ✢ ⲡⲓⲭⲱⲣⲓ ⲁⲃⲃⲁ ⲙⲱⲥⲏ

2. A sinner who went astray ✢ evil was all his way
   ✢ he drank sin like water ✢ ⲡⲓⲭⲱⲣⲓ ⲁⲃⲃⲁ ⲙⲱⲥⲏ

3. Satan blinded him with lust ✢ seduced him like the snake
   ✢ his eyes became blinded ✢ ⲡⲓⲭⲱⲣⲓ ⲁⲃⲃⲁ ⲙⲱⲥⲏ

4. He wondered, "Where is God? ✢ Is He found in this rock?
   ✢ On earth or in heaven?" ✢ ⲡⲓⲭⲱⲣⲓ ⲁⲃⲃⲁ ⲙⲱⲥⲏ

5. The Lord then called him ✢ leading him to *Šhehīt*
   ✢ and gave him a new life ✢ ⲡⲓⲭⲱⲣⲓ ⲁⲃⲃⲁ ⲙⲱⲥⲏ

6. He saw Abba Isidore ✢ and spoke about Jesus
   ✢ Christ, the Holy One ✢ ⲡⲓⲭⲱⲣⲓ ⲁⲃⲃⲁ ⲙⲱⲥⲏ

7. He put faith in his words ✢ and wept for his past life
   ✢ and became repentant ✢ ⲡⲓⲭⲱⲣⲓ ⲁⲃⲃⲁ ⲙⲱⲥⲏ

8. He met Abba Macarius ✢ and confessed with remorse
   ✢ so the Lord showed him a sign ✢ ⲡⲓⲭⲱⲣⲓ ⲁⲃⲃⲁ ⲙⲱⲥⲏ

9. Behold, an angel came ✢ carrying a black tablet
   ✢ and erased it to become white ✢ ⲡⲓⲭⲱⲣⲓ ⲁⲃⲃⲁ ⲙⲱⲥⲏ

Chapter Eight: Hymns

10. The Lord has heard your voice ⁜ He accepted all your tears

    ⁜ He erased all of your sins ⁜ ⲡⲓϫⲱⲣⲓ ⲁⲃⲃⲁ ⲙⲱⲥⲏ

11. His past, Jesus covered, ⁜ He forgave it by His blood

    ⁜ and forgot about it saying ⁜ ⲡⲓϫⲱⲣⲓ ⲁⲃⲃⲁ ⲙⲱⲥⲏ

12. A lion now a lamb ⁜ an example he became

    ⁜ the Lord's work is fulfilled ⁜ ⲡⲓϫⲱⲣⲓ ⲁⲃⲃⲁ ⲙⲱⲥⲏ

13. O faithful struggler ⁜ against the demonic wars

    ⁜ for many years passed by ⁜ ⲡⲓϫⲱⲣⲓ ⲁⲃⲃⲁ ⲙⲱⲥⲏ

14. They attacked you with your thoughts ⁜ with pride and self-image

    ⁜ and desires, day and night ⁜ ⲡⲓϫⲱⲣⲓ ⲁⲃⲃⲁ ⲙⲱⲥⲏ

15. He rejected to condemn ⁜ a monk who fell in sin

    ⁜ he said, "I am like him" ⁜ ⲡⲓϫⲱⲣⲓ ⲁⲃⲃⲁ ⲙⲱⲥⲏ

16. A teacher by example ⁜ he raised before the monks

    ⁜ a torn bag of some sand ⁜ ⲡⲓϫⲱⲣⲓ ⲁⲃⲃⲁ ⲙⲱⲥⲏ

17. He said, "These are my sins ⁜ the ignorance of my youth

    ⁜ my brother I should not judge" ⁜ ⲡⲓϫⲱⲣⲓ ⲁⲃⲃⲁ ⲙⲱⲥⲏ

18. O treasure of virtues ⁜ who conquered vain glory

    ⁜ and became very lowly ⁜ ⲡⲓϫⲱⲣⲓ ⲁⲃⲃⲁ ⲙⲱⲥⲏ

19. A monk in the fear of God ⁜ condemns his brother not

    ⁜ and looks toward heaven ⁜ ⲡⲓϫⲱⲣⲓ ⲁⲃⲃⲁ ⲙⲱⲥⲏ

20. As the father of fathers ✤ who stewards the strangers

    ✤ and gives so generously ✤ ⲡⲓϫⲱⲣⲓ ⲁⲃⲃⲁ ⲙⲱⲥⲏ

21. As Elijah in prayer ✤ when he needed water

    ✤ the heaven rained water ✤ ⲡⲓϫⲱⲣⲓ ⲁⲃⲃⲁ ⲙⲱⲥⲏ

22. Your words are a great treasure ✤ to every believer

    ✤ hermits and the worshipper ✤ ⲡⲓϫⲱⲣⲓ ⲁⲃⲃⲁ ⲙⲱⲥⲏ

23. On July first, a feast ✤ of a chosen martyr

    ✤ in the assembly of the just ✤ ⲡⲓϫⲱⲣⲓ ⲁⲃⲃⲁ ⲙⲱⲥⲏ

24. O martyr of Jesus Christ ✤ to you, praise is sweet

    ✤ with one voice we proclaim ✤ ⲡⲓϫⲱⲣⲓ ⲁⲃⲃⲁ ⲙⲱⲥⲏ

25. O the courageous Moses ✤ you are our role model

    ✤ with zeal in our life ✤ ⲡⲓϫⲱⲣⲓ ⲁⲃⲃⲁ ⲙⲱⲥⲏ

26. Visitors come to the abbey ✤ with heartfelt thanksgiving

    ✤ proclaiming and saying ✤ ⲡⲓϫⲱⲣⲓ ⲁⲃⲃⲁ ⲙⲱⲥⲏ

27. O blessing for the clergy ✤ O beloved of Jesus Christ

    ✤ living in Paradise ✤ ⲡⲓϫⲱⲣⲓ ⲁⲃⲃⲁ ⲙⲱⲥⲏ

28. In [city][189] and *Baramūs* ✤ brothers, monks and the priests

    ✤ all saying, "ⲁⲝⲓⲟⲥ" ✤ ⲡⲓϫⲱⲣⲓ ⲁⲃⲃⲁ ⲙⲱⲥⲏ

---

[189] The monks who composed this added "Texas" wherein lies St. Mary and Abba Moses Abbey, a Coptic monastery in the Diocese of the Southern United States.

29. Remember our Pope ✢ the beloved, Abba [ⲛⲓⲙ]

✢ and Abba [ⲛⲓⲙ][190], our bishop ✢ ⲡⲓϣⲱⲣⲓ ⲁⲃⲃⲁ ⲙⲱⲥⲏ

30. Likewise, I the sinner ✢ pray that I may be saved

✢ from my weaknesses and lusts, ✢ ⲡⲓϣⲱⲣⲓ ⲁⲃⲃⲁ ⲙⲱⲥⲏ

---

[190] Following the above footnote, Metropolitan Youssef became the shepherd of the diocese. In 1992, His Eminence was ordained as General Bishop and in 1993, His Eminence was appointed to care for the Coptic Diocese of the Southern United States. In 1995, His Grace was formally enthroned as the first Bishop of the Coptic Orthodox Diocese of the Southern United. Then in 2022, His Eminence was elevated to the rank of Metropolitan.

SALUTATIONS[191]

✚ Hail! O our holy father Abba Moses the Black, may his blessings be with us. Amen.

✚ Hail to you, O saint of God Abba Moses! Whom God had compassion on and planted in him good thoughts. He went to the place of Saint Abba Isidore.[192]

✚ Hail to you, O saint of God, O Abba Moses! Who completed the Apostle Paul's commandment and teaching that says, "Let us forsake the weapons of deception and let us be clothed by the weapons of righteousness and repentance" [2 Corinth 6:7]

✚ Hail to you, O saint of God! Who said, "O Savior of the world, who saved the thief crucified with [You], deliver me also, for I have fled unto You." [193]

✚ Hail to you, O saint of God, O Abba Moses! Who spent six years without sleeping during the night and who practiced devotion until he overcame the devil of fornication.[194]

---

[191] I adopted and revised the translation from Prof. Youhanna's publication, "Coptic and Arabic Liturgical texts relating to Moses the black", *ΣΥΝΑΞΙΣΚΑΘΟΛΙΚΗ. Beiträge zu Gottesdienst und Geschichte der fünf Patriarchate für Heinzgerd Brakmann zum 70* (2014): 751-766.
[192] §5
[193] §5
[194] §11

✢ Hail to you, O saint of God, O Abba Moses! Who regularly fasted and did not eat other than half a pound of dried bread with salt, and who prayed fifty prayers every day.[195]

✢ Hail to you, O saint of God, O Abba Moses! Whom God granted great grace, no longer fearing demons, but they became to him like passing flies.[196]

✢ Hail to you, O saint of God, O Abba Moses! In whom the Holy Spirit dwelled, and through whom crazy people were saved, demons were cast out from people, the sick were healed, and the Lord performed many wonders.[197]

✢ Hail to you, O saint of God, O Abba Moses! To whom God granted the priesthood and gathered five hundred brethren, monks in *Dayr al-Baramūs*.[198]

✢ Hail to you, O saint of God, O Abba Moses! Who rightfully received the Kingdom of Heaven.

✢ Hail to you, O saint of God, O Abba Moses! Who performed the commandments of the Lord Christ (glory be to Him) and pleased Him with your righteous deeds.

---

[195] §12 & §14
[196] §16
[197] §19
[198] §21

✦ Hail to you, O saint of God, O Abba Moses! Who became a perfect saint in Scetis, a virtuous priest, a spiritual father, and a mentor for the salvation of souls.

✦ Hail to you, O saint of God, O Abba Moses! Who attained martyrdom and completed your good fight on the 24th day of the month of *Ba'ūna*, in the peace of the Lord. Amen.

We beseech you, O our holy father, Abba Moses the Great, because of the passion you received for the sake of the name of Christ and the gifts He bestowed on you, just as the Lord Jesus Christ received you after your thievery, [that He] receive [us also] the sinners, and intercede for [us] before the Lord Christ to save [us] from the trials of the devil, that He may forgive [our] sins, granting [us] a share in the Kingdom of Heaven with you, by your accepted prayers before Him through all ages.

BIBLIOGRAPHY

'Abd al-Massīḥ, Yassa. "Doxologies in the Coptic Church: Unedited Bohairic Doxologies (Tûbah – An- Nâsi)." *BSAC 11* (1945): 95–158.

Abdelsayed, Fr John Paul (now Bishop Kyrillos). *The Strong Saint Abba Moses.* California: Saint Paul Brotherhood Press, 2010.

'Abd al-Massīḥ Ṣalīb al-Baramūsī al-Masʿūdī (Editor). *Kitāb al- ḫulaji al-muqaddas [The Book of the Holy Euchologion].* Cairo, 1902.

al-Anbā Mattāūs w-al-Anbā Ṣamūʾīl. *al-Ibṣāliyāt al-Wāṭus w-al-Adām. Baramhāt - al-Šhahr al-Ṣaġīr [The Adam and Watos Psalis for Paramhotep and the short month] vol. 2.* Cairo: 1994.

al-Qiddīs Ǧīrūm [St Jerome]. *Ṯhlāṯh Siyyar Biqalam al-Qiddīs Ǧīrūm: al-Anbā Būlā Awal al-Sawāḥ, al-Qiddīs Hīlāriyūn, al-Qiddīs Malḫūs al-Rāhib al-Asīr [Three Biographies by St Jerome: St Paul the Hermit, St Hilary, and St Malchus the Monk].* Fr Yūḥanā ʿAṭā Maḥrūs (Translator). Cairo: Alexandria School, 2019.

Allies, Mary H (Translator). *Leaves from St. John Chrysostom.* South Carolina: BiblioBazaar, 2009.

'Aṭṭālla Arsaniyūs al-Muḥarraqī. ⲠⲰⲘ ⲚϯⲘⲈⲦⲢⲈϤϢⲈⲘϢⲒ ⲚⲦⲈ ⲠⲒⲆⲒⲀⲔⲰⲚ ⲚⲈⲘ ⲚⲒⲂⲰⲢⲈⲘ *[The book of the service of deacon and hymns].* Cairo, 1973.

Amélineau, Emile. *De Historia Lausiaca quaenam sit hujus ad monachorum aegyptiorum historiam scribendam utilitas: adjecta sunt quaedam hujus Historiae coptica fragmenta inedita.* E. Leroux, 1887.

Amélineau, Emile. *La Géographie de l'Egypte à l'époque copte.* Paris, 1893.

Amélineau, Emile. *Monuments pour servir à l'histoire de d'Égypte chrétienne: histoire des monastères de la Basse-Égypte; vies des saints Paul, Antoine, Macaire, Maxime et Domèce Jean Le Main, etc. Vol. 25.* E. Leroux, 1894.

Arsānyūs al-Muḥarraqī, ⲡϫⲱⲙ ⲛⲧⲉ ⲛⲓϣⲓⲛϯϣⲟⲩ ⲉⲑⲩ̄ ⲛ̄ϯⲡⲁⲣⲑⲉⲛⲟⲥ ⲛⲓⲁⲅⲅⲉⲗⲟⲥ ⲛⲓⲁⲡⲟⲥⲧⲟⲗⲟⲥ ⲛⲓⲙⲁⲣⲧⲩⲣⲟⲥ ⲛⲉⲙ ⲛⲏⲉⲑⲟⲩⲁⲃ [*the book of the holy veneration of the Virgin, angels, apostles, martyrs, and the saints*]. Cairo, 1972.

Aubert, Jean-Jacques. "La pertinence de la négritude: Moïse l'Ethiopien." *Histoire et herméneutique. Mélanges offerts à G. Hammann,* vol. 3 (Labor et Fides, 2002): 27-40.

Basset, René. "Mois de Toubeh et d'Amchir." *PO Tome 11* (1915): 609-614.

Basset, Rene (editor). *Le synaxaire arabe jacobite (rédaction copte) V. Les mois de Baounah, Abib, Mesoré et jours complémentaires*. PO 17 (Paris 1923): 591–594.

Budge, Wallis E.A. *The Paradise of the Fathers V. II Containing the Counsels of the Holy Men and Questions & Answers of the Ascetic Brethren Generally known as the Sayings of the Fathers of Egypt*. London: Chatto & Windus, 1907.

Bishop Epiphanius. *Bustān ar-Ruhbān*. Cairo: St Macarius Monastery, 2014.

Bishop Makarios. *al-Qawī al-Qidīs al-Anbā Mūsa al-Aswad*. Cario, 2006.

Brakke, David. *Demons and the making of the monk: spiritual combat in early Christianity*. Harvard University Press, 2009.

Bowman, Alan K. *Egypt after the Pharaohs, 332 BC-AD 642: from Alexander to the Arab Conquest*. University of California Press, 1996.

Bunge, Gabriel. "Palladiana: I. Introduction aux fragments coptes de l'Histoire Lausiaque." *Studia Monastica 32* (1990): 79–129.

Butler, Alban. *The Lives of the Fathers, Martyrs, and Other Principal Saints: Compiled from Original Monuments and Other Authentic Records, Illustrated with the Remarks of Judicious Modern Critics and Historians*. London: John Murphy, 1812.

Chaîne, Marius. *Le Manuscrit de la version copte en dialecte sahidique des "Apophthegmata Patrum."* Le Caire: Impr. de l'Institut français d'archéologie orientale, 1960.

Bibliography

Cheikho, Louis. "Catalogue raisonné des manuscrits de la Bibliothèque orientale. V. Patristique, conciles, écrivains ecclésiastiques anciens, hagiologie." *Mélanges de l'Université Saint-Joseph, tome 11*. 1926.

Chitty, Derwas J. "Abba Isaiah." *The Journal of Theological Studies*, Volume XXII, Issue I (Oxford University Press, April 1971): 47–72. https://doi.org/10.1093/jts/XXII.I.47

Chryssaygis, John and Pachomios Penkett (Translators). *Abba Isaiah of Scetis: Ascetic Discourses*. MI: Cistercian Publications, 2002.

Clarke, William Kemp Lowther. *The Lausiac History*. London, 1918.

Coptic Encyclopedia. Edited by Karen J. Torjesen, Gawdat Gabra, and Hany N. Takla: https://ccdl.claremont.edu/digital/collection/cce -Archbishop Basilios. "Martyrdom."

Crum, Walter E. *A Coptic Dictionary*. Oxford: Clarendon Press, 1939.

Devos, Paul. "Saint Jean Cassien et saint Moïse l'Éthiopien." *Analecta Bollandiana 103*, no. 1-2 (1985): 61-74.

Dūmādiyūs al-Baramūsī. ⲡϫⲱⲙ ⲛ̄ⲧⲉ ⲛⲓϫⲓⲛϯⲱⲟⲩ ⲉⲑ︤ⲩ︥ ⲛ̄ϯⲡⲁⲣⲑⲉⲛⲟⲥ ⲛⲓⲁⲅⲅⲉⲗⲟⲥ ⲛⲓⲁⲡⲟⲥⲧⲟⲗⲟⲥ ⲛⲓⲙⲁⲣⲧⲩⲣⲟⲥ ⲛⲉⲙ ⲛⲏⲉⲑ︤ⲩ︥ [The book of the holy venerations of the Virgin, angels, apostles, martyrs and saints]. Cairo: 1922.

Feltoe, Charles L. (Translator). *St. Dionysius of Alexandria: Letters and Treatises*. London – New York: The Macmillan Company, 1918.

Fīlūthā'us al-Maqqārī (Editor). *al-Kitāb al-ibṣaliyat w-al-turuhat al-watos w-al-ādām [The Book of Psalis and Explanations, both Watos and Adam]*. Cairo, 1913.

Gabra, Gawdat. *Coptic Monasteries: Egypt's Monastic Art and Architecture*. Oxford University Press, 2002.

Gabra, Gawdat. "Dair Anba Musa al-Aswad: das originale Baramus Kloster in Wadi al-Natrun." *BSAC 36* (1997): 72-73

Genghini, Maria G. "'Go, sit in your cell, and your cell will teach you everything' (AP Moses 6): How the Physical Environment Shaped the Spirituality of Early Egyptian Monasticism." In *Studia Patristica. Vol. XCI: Papers Presented At the Seventeenth International Conference On Patristic Studies Held In Oxford 2015*, ed., Markus Vinzent. Leuven: Peeters, 2017.

Graf, Georg. *Catalogue de manuscrits arabes chrétiens conservés au Caire*. Biblioteca Apostolica Vaticana, Città del Vaticano, 1934.

Graf, Georg. *Geschichte der christlichen arabischen Literatur*. 5 vols. (Studi e Testi 118, 133, 146, 147,172). Città del Vaticano: Biblioteca Apostolica Vaticana, 1944-1953.

Grossmann, Peter, and Hans-Georg Severin. "Zum antiken Bestand der al-Adrâ'kirche des Dair al-Baramûs im Wâdi Natrûn." (1997).

Hedstrom, Darlene B. L. "Your cell will teach you all things": The relationship between monastic practice and the architectural design of the cell in Coptic monasticism, 400–1000. (Ph.D. Diss, Miami University, Department of History, 2001).

Helmy, Mickel (editor and translator). *ad-Difnār: al-Āntīfūnāriyūn aṣ-Ṣaʿīdī*. Cairo: Alexandria School, 2018.

Innemee, Karel C. "Deir al-Baramūs, excavations at the so-called site of Moses the Black, 1994-1999." *BSAC 39* (2000): 123-135.

Innemme, Karel C. "Excavations at the site of Deir Al-Baramūs 2002-2005." *BSAC 44* (2005): 55–68.

John Climacus. *The Ladder of Divine Ascent*. Translated by Archimandrite Lazarus Moore. Boston, Massachusetts: Holy Transfiguration Monastery, 2012.

Lett Feltoe, Charles (translator). *St. Dionysius of Alexandria: Letters and Treatises*. London – New York: The Macmillan Company, 1918.

Macomber, William F. *Catalogue of Christian Arabic Manuscripts of the Franciscan Centre of Christian Oriental Studies*. Cairo, 1984.

O'Leary, De Lacy. *The Difnar (Antiphonarium) of the Coptic Church, Vol. 3: Bashons, Baounah, Abib, Mesre and the intercalary days or Nasi*. London, 1930.

O'Leary, De Lacy. *The saints of Egypt in the Coptic calendar*. London – New York, 1937.

Mikhail, Maged S and Tim Vivian, "Zacharias of Sakha: An Encomium on the Life of John the Little." *Coptic Church Review 18*, no 1-2 (1997): 1-64.

Mīnā al-Miḥalāwī al-Baramūsī (Editor). ⲡⲓϫⲱⲙ ⲛⲧⲉ ϯⲯⲁⲗⲙⲟⲇⲓⲁ ⲉⲑⲟⲩⲁⲃ ⲛⲧⲉⲙⲣⲟⲙⲡⲓ *[The Book of the Holy Annual Psalmodia]*. Cairo: Monastery of al-Baramūs, reprinted 2017.

Moderan, Y. "Mazices, Mazaces." *Encyclopédie berbère* 31 (2010): 4799-4810.

Molinier, Jean-Luc. "Abba Moïse l'Éthiopien, moine de Scété, et sa trajectoire de sanctification." *Collectanea Cisterciensia* 77, no. 4 (2015): 343-367.

Nessim, Shady K. *The Life of Sts Maximus and Dometius: Monastery, Hymnography, Iconography*. St Shenouda Press, 2022.

Noell, Brian. "Race in Late Antique Egypt: Moses the Black and Authentic Historical Voice." *Eras* 6 (2004).

Paczkowski, Celestyn Mieczysław. "Amalek and the Amalekites in the Ancient Christian Literature." *Teologia Cztowiek* 26.2 (Nicolaus Copernicus University: Toruń, 2014): 137–160.

Pazis, Marguerite (Editor). *Festal Vespers Hymns: 17 January, St Anthony the Great, Holy Heiromartyr and Founder of Monasticism*. Greek Orthodox Patriarchate of Alexandria and all Africa, 29 December 2018.

Pirone, Bartholomew (ed., and trans.). "Vita di Mosè l'Etiope." *Studia Orientalia Christiana Collectanea* 24 (Cairo–Jerusalem 1991): 7–115.

Regnault, Lucien. *Abbé Isaïe. Recueil ascétique: Introduction et traduction française par les moines des Solesmes*. Bégrolles: Abbaye de Bellefontaine, 1970.

Robert E. Sinkewicz (translator). *Evagrius of Pontus: The Greek Ascetic Corpus*. Oxford University Press, 2003.

Ṣamū'īl al-Suryānī. al-Ādyurah al-Maṣriyah al-'Āmerah. Cairo, 1968.

Sheridan, Mark. *Rufus of Shotep: Homilies on the Gospels of Matthew and Luke; introduction, text, translation, commentary*. Roma: CIM, 1998.

Siegfried G, Richter. "The Beginnings of Christianity in Nubia", in Gawdat Gabra (ed.), *Christianity and Monasticism in Aswan and Nubia* (Cairo, 2013; online edn, Cairo Scholarship Online, 18 Sept. 2014):

https://doi.org/10.5743/cairo/9789774165610.003.0006, accessed 28 Oct. 2022.

Simaika, Marcus. *Catalogue of the Coptic and Arabic Manuscripts in the Coptic Museum, the Patriarchate, the Principal Churches of Cairo and Alexandria and the Monasteries of Egypt, vol. 1*. Cairo, 1939.

Sinkewicz E, Robert (translator). *Evagrius of Pontus: The Greek Ascetic Corpus*. Oxford University Press, 2003.

Suciu, Alin. "Sitting in the cell: the literary development of an ascetic praxis in Paul of Tamma's writings. With an edition of some hitherto unknown fragments of De cella." In *The Journal of Theological Studies 68*, no. 1 (2017): 141-171.

Starodubcev, Tatjana. "St. Moses the Ethiopian or the Black. Cult and representation in the Middle Ages." *Zograf 43* (2019): 1-22.

Troupeu, Gérard. *Catalogue des manuscrits arabes ; première partie : manuscrits chrétiens, tome I*. Parigi, 1972.

Walford, Edward. *History of the Church by Sozomen and Philostorgius*. London: John Childs and Son, Bungay, 1855.

Ward, Benedicta (translator). *The sayings of the desert fathers: the alphabetical collection*. Kentucky: Cistercian Publishing, 1975.

White, Evelyn H.G. *The monasteries of the Wâdi'n Natrûn vol. II the History of the Monasteries of Nitria and Scetis*. Arno Press, 1926.

Wicker, O'Brien K. "Ethiopian Moses" (collected sources). *Ascetic behavior in Greco-Roman antiquity*, ed., V. L. Wimbush (Minneapolis 1990): 329–348.

Wortley, John. *An Introduction to the Desert Fathers*. UK: Cambridge University Press, 2019.

Wortley, John. *Give me a Word: The Alphabetical Sayings of the Desert Fathers*. New York: SVS Press, 2014.

Wortley, John. *The anonymous sayings of the desert fathers: A select edition and complete English translation*. New York: Cambridge University Press, 2013.

Wortley, John. *More Sayings of the Desert Fathers: An English Translation and Notes*. UK: Cambridge University Press, 2019.

Valantasis, Richard, Douglas K. Bleyle, and Dennis C. Haugh. *The Gospels and Christian Life in History and Practice*. Maryland: Rowman & Littlefield Publishers, 2009.

Vivian, Tim and Apostolos Athanassakis (translators). *The Life of Antony: The Coptic Life and Greek Life*. MI: Cistercian Publications, 2003.

Vivian, Tim. *St. Macarius the Spirit-bearer: Coptic Texts Relating to Saint Macarius the Great*. New York: St. Vladimir's Seminary Press, 2004.

Youssef, Youhanna N. *Aḍwā' 'ala ar-Rahbana al-Qibṭiyya*. Cairo: Alexandria School, 2018.

Youssef, Youhanna N. "Coptic and Arabic Liturgical texts relating to Moses the black." *ΣΥΝΑΞΙΣ ΚΑΘΟΛΙΚΗ. Beiträge zu Gottesdienst und Geschichte der fünf Patriarchate für Heinzgerd Brakmann zum 70* (2014): 751-766.

Zoega, Georgio. *Catalogus codicum Copticorum manu scriptorum qui in Museo Borgiano Velitris adservantur*. Roma, 1810.

www.ingramcontent.com/pod-product-compliance
Lightning Source LLC
Chambersburg PA
CBHW031631160426
43196CB00006B/363